Martyn Johnson was a 'beat bobby' with Sheffield City Police Force for years before he was seconded to CID. After two years, he found that he missed grass-roots policing and returned to the beat for a further seven years. He lives in Wentworth village, South Yorkshire, with his wife, Christine.

Also by Martyn Johnson

What's Tha Up To? Memories of a Yorkshire Bobby

WHAT'S THA UP TO NAH?

A Yorkshire Bobby's Life on the Beat

Martyn Johnson

sphere

SPHERE

First published in Great Britain in 2011 by Wharncliffe Local History,
an imprint of Pen & Sword Books Ltd
This edition published in 2012 by Sphere

A CIP catalogue record for this book
is available from the British Library.

ISBN 978-0-7515-4964-5

Typeset in Goudy by M Rules
Printed and bound in Great Britain by
Clays Ltd, St Ives plc

Papers used by Sphere are from well-managed forests
and other responsible sources.

MIX
Paper from
responsible sources
FSC
www.fsc.org   FSC® C104740

Sphere
An imprint of
Little, Brown Book Group
100 Victoria Embankment
London EC4Y 0DY

An Hachette UK Company
www.hachette.co.uk

www.littlebrown.co.uk

I dedicate this book to my wonderful parents, Esther and Fred Johnson, and also to my mother- and father-in-law, Mabel and Albert Mills, who drew the short straw when I married their daughter, Christine.

Contents

Foreword

by Catherine Bailey
Author of *Black Diamonds*

Martyn Johnson is a fabulous storyteller. I was lucky enough to hear some of these stories – and some of those that appeared in his first book, *What's Tha Up To?* – as we drove for miles and miles around South Yorkshire.

In researching my own book, *Black Diamonds*, Martyn was my guide. I owe him a huge debt: he took me to places that I wouldn't otherwise have seen and introduced me to people that I would never have met. Above all, he brought the past back to life: through him, I glimpsed what it was like to grow up and work in a colliery village.

These stories, and others he told me about his life as a 'bobby' in the tough East End of Sheffield in the early

1960s and 1970s, are a nostalgic reminder of how things have changed and they opened my eyes. Some made me laugh; others brought me close to tears. They are extraordinary stories and I am sure you will enjoy them.

Introduction and Acknowledgements

All this started when I was relating some of my memories of being in the police force to my youngest son, Paul. 'Dad, why don't you write these stories down so that we can show them to your grandkids and then they will know what life in the old days was like?' His brother and sister, Richard and Sally, both agreed and badgered me to get on with it.

I thought and thought about what he had said and, to be honest, I wasn't feeling too great health-wise at the time and so decided to put pen to paper just in case something happened to me. It sounds a bit dramatic, I know, but that's how it all started and the stories were turned into a book called *What's Tha Up To?*.

To my utter amazement the book was well received. I didn't think it would sell ten copies, let alone several thousand, and it went on to to reprint three times in its first year. It is still selling well. I remain absolutely staggered at the response. Within the first few weeks I was receiving mail and email from expatriates throughout the world and all the letters were saying the same thing: that the book was full of nostalgia and made people both laugh and cry, and to please get on with another book quickly. The same comments came from different people who reviewed the book both in the newspapers, magazines and on the Internet, where there are some very kind reviews.

I also received some wonderful comments from old colleagues as well as from serving police officers all over the country. By the time you read this, *What's Tha Up To?* will be on sale on a national basis, not just locally.

I was asked at one point if I wanted a 'ghost writer', to which I replied, 'Nay, I'm sure the readers would prefer it written by someone with a bit of life in them.' With the help of my friend and editor Brian Elliott, the second book, *What's Tha Up To Nah?* has been published and I thank, in no small part, my publishing company Pen and Sword Ltd and the lovely group of girls in the office, but mainly Emma Howe, who I have worked with the closest.

The police force, as we all know, has changed an awful lot in the last fifty years and I think that this is one of the reasons why the book has caused so much interest, not just in England but also abroad.

I would like at this time to thank the thousands of people who have bought *What's Tha Up To?* and have communicated to me their support. Thanks once more to Brian Elliott, my editor, for his faith in me by allowing me to write the book myself and in my own way; it can't have been easy for him dealing with a man with only one brain cell, but nevertheless he has stuck with me. Thank you Brian.

I would also like to thank my good friend Catherine Bailey, the author of *Black Diamonds*, who I worked with on her book for three years. You are an inspiration Catherine, and I am very grateful for you writing the foreword to the new book.

As a result of the first book I have, thankfully, met and been in touch with people who I thought were long gone. George 'Jud' Proctor, my old mentor, got in touch with me from Skegness and both our families met there after many years apart. Unfortunately George passed away at the age of eighty-nine a few months after we had met again and I was extremely proud to have been asked to do part of his eulogy at his funeral in Skegness.

I was also allowed to meet Barbara Greaves, our old Attercliffe telephonist at the hospital, two days before she passed away in her eighties. What a wonderful lady.

I would also like to thank the following for their support: Mrs Lynn Eyre (Australia); Jennifer Beaumont (Australia); Mary McConnie (Trinidad and Tobago); Mary and Terry Watson; Bud and Murial Leggitt and Vera

(Canada); Joy Malin (South Africa); Jaap Stoof (Holland); Avand and Tune Friedrickson (Norway); Michael Boyles (Wales); The Red Arrows Flying Display Team and for their wonderful signed picture wishing me all the best with *What's Tha Up To Nah?*; Paul Chadwick; Pat Levesley; Chris Mann; Mr Fletcher (my old bank manager); Jean and Roy Williamson; Tony and Theresa Garnett; Robert ('Geordie') Clarkson and Eileen; Steve Edwards (Police Federation); Peter and Anne Cooke; Tom and Eileen Locker; former Sheffield teacher Dave Pyle (for his literary praise); Ian Hempsell; Ralph and Norma; Peter Spencer; Paul Licence and Debbie (*Sheffield Star* Newspapers); Lesley Webster; Maria de Souza and Sue Walker (Off the Shelf Festival of Writing and Reading, Sheffield); Fiona and Mike Swann; Sheila 'Crofty' McMillan and husband, John; Irene Proctor and all the members of George and Irene's family, especially Vera ('Sandy') Sanderson-Key for putting us back in touch with the Proctor family; South Yorkshire Police Helicopter Team; Bronnie and John Beever; Elizabeth and Geoff Lister; Julie Marsden; Jilly and Derek Gennard. I would also like to thank poet Ian McMillan, the Barnsley Bard.

Thanks also to: Michael Bond, Rachel and Paul Johnson, Amanda and Richard Johnson, Sally Johnson and Michael 'Woody' Woodhall, Mavis and Gordon Palmer, Christine and Mick Naylor and Florence Newton. Oh, and of course my dear wife Christine, for all her support and secretarial skills.

Lack of space precludes me from listing everyone, but you know who you are and you are certainly not forgotten: my thanks go to you all.

CHAPTER ONE

The Law of the Jungle

C rash – the sound of breaking glass was unmistakable.
It was my twentieth birthday and I was working a
foot beat in the coldest winter since records began, 1962–3.
I had been a beat bobby in the tough area of Attercliffe in
Sheffield for nearly a year and, because of the bitter cold and
heavy snow, I wished I'd joined the French Foreign Legion in
the desert instead; at least they were warm. I was very much
a 'rookie' bobby and still wet behind the ears.

I'd started my night shift at 11pm and worked my way up
the main Attercliffe Road, checking the front and rear of
shop premises looking for any signs of burglary. All had been
quiet until I heard the crash of breaking glass coming from
somewhere nearby, but where? The last property I was going
to check before heading back to the nick for my snap was a

garage that sold cars, about fifty yards or so in front of me, near the railway bridge.

Within two minutes of hearing the sound of breaking glass I was there at the garage. The light from the gas lamp twenty yards away was insufficient to assess the situation and so, reluctantly, I switched my torch on. Sure enough, there were jemmy or crowbar marks near the door lock where someone had tried to force it open. The bottom of the glass door had been kicked in and broken glass could be seen strewn across the office floor within the premises.

Racing to the rear of the premises revealed a large window which, although fairly high up, was open. A good burglar, having broken in, makes an alternative exit should he find himself trapped. If he was still in the premises – as I hoped that he would be – I was going to have difficulty containing him and would have to somehow stop him escaping.

There were very few burglar alarms in those days but, even though these premises had one, it wasn't going off which amazed me because I knew that inside was a fairly large safe – and I was betting that Burglar Bill knew that as well.

There were no police radios or mobile phones fifty years ago, and the nearest phone kiosk was half a mile away. At 2am there were no passing cars to stop and ask to send for assistance. Do I wait at the rear of the garage in case he climbed out of the window, or do I stand at the front? He had three options: climb out of the rear window, exit

8

through the front door or stay put. I'd had to use my torch to check the door and windows, so whoever was inside must know I was there. I also knew that he'd got a jemmy or crowbar in his possession. I was on my own but knew that I would have to face him, something I didn't fancy, but it had to be done.

From hearing the glass break to now would have been three to four minutes so, for my money, he was still inside and I was getting paid £10 4s a week to catch burglars.

Helmet on the floor, I took off my cape and spread it over the bottom half of the door frame and at the same time tried to cover as much of the broken glass inside as the length of the cape would allow. He must still be inside, but I couldn't spot him with the aid of the metal police-issue lamp.

Although part of the job, it was still unnerving and my heart was nearly jumping out of my chest. I didn't want to be kicked in the face as I clambered part way through the door, so I had to be quick and hope that I would avoid some of the jagged pieces of glass in the door frame at the same time.

I was almost through the door when the expression 'a pain in the arse' came to mind, as I felt a large sliver of glass stab the right cheek of my bum. The adrenalin kicked in as I jumped up and found a light switch. The light was dazzling as I checked first one office and then the other, but both were empty. 'Bloody hell I've missed him!' I said to myself.

A sudden scraping noise behind me made me spin round. I'd not seen the door saying 'toilet' on it. I grabbed the handle, kicked the door hard and made for the light switch as the door shot open. Bingo, there he was, head and shoulders halfway through the window frame at the back of the building. There was no escape for him, but I also saw the crowbar in his left hand.

As I went to grab his legs to pull him backwards, he swung his foot which hit me in the chest, and a second kick caught me on the side of my face and knocked me back. Another go at grabbing his legs produced the same result and I was kicked in the face again. He wasn't going to come with me without a struggle. Another approach was needed so I reached up and grabbed his jersey collar with my left hand, and with my right hand I made contact with two small round objects which, for some unknown reason, as I gently squeezed them made him very vocal in a squeaky sort of way. Luckily for me he dropped the crowbar at the same time.

With a struggle I managed to drag him to the front office and held him face down on the desk with his arm behind his back. He was desperate to get away and I assumed that he'd got 'form' (previous convictions) and didn't want to lose his freedom. What a nightmare: I couldn't get him out of the front door, which was locked, and I couldn't let go of him to get my handcuffs out or use the garage phone either and I was using up all my energy just restraining him. After a few minutes of tussling I was worn out, but luckily for me at that point several things happened together. The alarm bell on the outside of the building started to ring and I also saw the reflection of a flashing blue light. Two policemen in flat hats (Road Traffic officers) arrived at the front of the building, quickly followed by two more. Seeing my predicament, the two officers crawled carefully through the hole in the door and cuffed the man with the sore knackers, and at this time the divisional car, a Hillman Husky Shooting Brake, arrived with Inspector Fred Jacques and his driver. They sent for the keyholder to the premises, who later unlocked the door so that the prisoner could be taken to Attercliffe nick to be interviewed by the CID lads.

When they took him away, even though my face was hurting, I had to smile because he was wearing a black-and-white striped jumper just like a cartoon burglar. He was also wearing his socks on his hands to avoid leaving fingerprints. This was a sure sign that he'd been in trouble before, which he had, and he ended up with another six months in the 'slammer' (prison).

I couldn't understand why all the lads and the gaffer had arrived together, but I was certainly glad they had.

Apparently, and unbeknownst to me as a rookie, when some alarms were activated a signal was sent to the police station and the alarm bell on the premises remained silent on a set delay time of ten minutes. This allowed as many police cars to surround the building as possible before the alarm became audible, thus giving them more chance to catch the culprit. If I'd known that, I wouldn't have ended up with a chunk of glass in my backside!

Around twelve years after this incident I was working 3pm to 11pm at Darnall sub-station. It had been a fairly quiet shift; starting with taking the kids from Whitby Road School across the road on their way home.

I loved the kids and Sheffield people in general. Being a beat bobby was, to me, the most satisfying job in the world. The banter and chat with kids and people was brilliant. Many times I have heard people say that you'll have no friends as a policeman. How wrong they were. If you were right with them, they were right with you. When I first joined I didn't know a soul in Sheffield and neither did I know where to get a cuppa on the beat. Things were very different now: a bacon sarnie here, a cuppa there and a pint at the back door of a pub if I wanted one.

The more people I knew the more I got to know. I think they call it networking now and the younger end think they've found something new with Facebook and Twitter. Never mind Facebook and Twitter, go out today and talk to someone you don't know face to face, nine times out of ten it will give you pleasure and the same for them as well. Just try – you never know you may enjoy it.

Darnall Terminus was fairly quiet for a Saturday night and I was looking forward to having a couple of pints after work with Harold and Maureen, the stewards at the Conservative Club.

It was about 10.50pm and only ten minutes to go until the end of the shift. As I approached the police sub-station on Senior Road, I heard a commotion behind me on Greenland Road. A small group of men were coming towards me. I could see that they were agitated and one of them shouted, 'Ring for an ambulance.' I opened the door of the sub-station and switched on the light and the men followed me in.

As I looked I could see a man aged about seventy and his face was covered in blood – what a mess. Whilst using the internal phone to call an ambulance, I looked at him again and got a shock. He was Ted, a retired steelworker who I used to chat with. He always reminded me of my own dad to look at, but somehow he appeared different now and then I realised why. Most of his nose was missing and there was blood everywhere, poor chap.

The ambulance must have been close by as it arrived no longer than two minutes after my call and Ted was taken to the hospital. One of the men who brought Ted to the station told me that he had been walking behind him across the Terminus. Coming towards them both was a big chap of about thirty-five and poor old Ted accidentally bumped into him, apologising at the same time for doing so. Ted then kept on walking but the big bloke went after him, spun him round and started thumping him in the face and chest. The witness then saw him put his face to Ted's and bite his nose clean off.

Just then the phone rang; it was the night duty sergeant at Attercliffe. 'Johnson, are you dealing with a bad assault at Darnall?' he said.

'Yes, Sergeant,' I replied.

'A chap's rung in from a payphone at Darnall. He says if you're on duty he wants to talk to you. I'll put him through.'

'Martyn, a nutter's just come into the Wellington pub and he's covered in blood.' It was Norman who worked at a local scrapyard; we sometimes had a beer together. Although he was a bit of a lad, he also had his own ideas of right and wrong and he was okay. He wouldn't have phoned me to grass a thief up.

'Who is he?' I asked.

'Cowardly Savage' (I'd love to put his real name).

'I'm on my way. I'll be there in three minutes, thanks,' I replied.

The name he'd given me was that of the bloke I had caught breaking into the garage years ago. Although I'd had no dealings with him since then, he'd been in and out of prison many times, mainly for violence. If he was the bloke that smashed up poor old Ted and then had bitten off his nose, I couldn't wait to have a not-too-friendly chat with him. I was there in a flash.

As I walked through the front door of the pub someone shouted, 'Look out!' I heard a whoosh and a thud near my face as something shot passed me. I looked to my left and there, embedded in the door frame, was a small meat cleaver, right at the side of my face. For what seemed like an eternity I just froze on the spot and then I saw Mr Cowardly Savage standing at the bar with a broken bottle in his hand. He was covered in blood and just stood there glaring at me.

I was shaking, not with fear – that happens later when you've had time to think and reflect. I was shaking with anger that he'd nearly done for me as well as poor old Ted and for that he was going to pay. As I set off for him someone shouted, 'The bleeding bastard's just bit old Ted's nose off.' At the same time he smashed a bar stool over Mr Cowardly Savage's head and he went down like a sack of spuds. If he'd hit him with the seat end of the stool and not the legs he may have been a goner – how sad.

By the time I'd arrived at the pub it was about 11.10pm, the end of supping up time, so there were only half a dozen lads still there and they were ready for leaving. When they heard what had happened to old Ted, who they knew, all hell was let loose and they were on top of laddo like a flash. Unfortunately, at that moment a speck of dust flew into my eye and it took a couple of minutes before I could see properly again.

A couple of minutes ago I'd wanted to rip him apart, but now I had to stop the lads from doing the same, what a shame. The landlord, who was new to the pub, must have rung the station asking for assistance and three of the night-shift lads arrived, as did the Black Maria (prison van) from West Bar police station. I winked at the lads in the pub and nodded my head towards the door. Norman 'the stool juggler' and the other lads knew what I meant and legged it; no one had seen a thing and there were no witnesses as to what had happened with the stool.

He was handcuffed and locked up after admitting the assaults. Knowing that he would be banged up for a few years, he also asked for a few burglaries to be TIC'd (taken into consideration). This was a way of admitting to other crimes and wiping his slate clean, without additional punishment. A guilty plea followed and he went to prison for four or five years.

Poor old Ted's life was ruined. Having worked hard all his life and after seeing active service in the Second World War, to be attacked in such a brutal and cowardly way by someone who, in my opinion, wasn't worth snap or baccy, was unforgivable. I am not a hard man but on occasions like this, concerning a savage attack on a poor defenceless old man, I would like to see the stocks back again. There are far too many 'do-gooders and jobsworths' who haven't seen incidents like this at first hand and I'm sure they'd change their tune if it happened to them or their relative. From what I can gather these days there are more organisations dealing with prisoners' rights than with the victims' rights. What a barmy world we live in. In my day, muggings and assaults of old people were almost unheard of, and rare incidents like the one described were dealt with swiftly and in a manner befitting the crime, by people who themselves had been in trouble in the past. Even to them, attacks like that were totally taboo.

Now and again I took Ted for a pint, but he was reluctant because of his permanent disfigurement. He was well liked and respected and I was later told that some of the likely lads, who themselves had done time in prison, made sure that while laddo was in prison he got his comeuppance. Don't ask me how; I wasn't told. I didn't need to know, but I'm sure that he'd have been given a beating now and then with the following words ringing in his ears: 'That's for poor old Ted.'

CHAPTER TWO

The Hair of the Dog

Ask anyone who knew 'The Cliffe' in the early 1960s whether it was ever quiet on a Saturday night and I know what the answer would be: 'Da must be jokin,' or 'No bleedin' chance.'

All the lights in the pubs were on and it was 11pm and closing time. I was standing at the side of the police box on Attercliffe Road at its junction with Staniforth Road and, apart from the occasional sound of a car going slowly past, there was very little noise. A few people were leaving the notorious Dog and Partridge pub across the road from where I stood, but even they were quiet; no laughter, shouting, screaming or swearing as they scuttled off home as fast as they could. I heard the front doors of the Dog and the Carlton pubs close and the noise of the bolts being slid across, locks turning and then all was quiet: it was amazing.

It was January 1963 and even though Attercliffe usually got less snow than other parts of the city it was getting its fair share now. Through the blizzard I could make out another bobby crossing the road towards me and I knew it was Jeff Loukes, who was working the beat on the other side of Attercliffe Road. Jeff was an old-timer and a nicer guy you couldn't wish to meet. He was a wise old owl and, like most of the other lads, he didn't miss a trick. At that time I hardly knew anyone in Sheffield and every now and then Jeff and his lovely wife, May, would take me out with them for a pint or two. The snow was really coming down and Jeff said that it was the worst he'd seen down The Cliffe since 1947–8. After a crafty fag in the police box, or Tardis as some people now call it, we rejoined our respective beats.

The front and back doors of all the shops had to be checked on every beat, to make sure they were secure or hadn't been broken into. Depending on the size of the beat, they had to be checked once before and once after mealtime. This kept us on our toes all night, especially when some of the crafty old sergeants would fasten a strand of wool across a passageway. If they found that the wool had not been broken, you'd not checked the rear of the property concerned and then you could get fined £1 for neglect of duty.

Because the snow was now so deep, walking was hard work and, even though it was freezing, I was sweating. I was down near Washford Bridge, where it crossed the River Don, and found it strange that only 200 years ago the River Don at this point would have been teeming with salmon (hence the local place-name Salmon Pastures) trying to run up the Mill Race.

It was about 1.30am now and the snow was thick and falling faster than ever. The conditions were that bad that there was nothing in the way of traffic on this, the main road between Sheffield and Rotherham; and I knew that I would have to walk back to my digs when I finished work at 7am as the buses would not be running.

I was making my way back to Whitworth Lane police station about a mile away when, through the blizzard, I could make out someone walking towards me dressed in a long coat and a flat hat like the ones bus drivers would wear. It obviously wasn't Jeff or he'd have a helmet and a cape on, just like me. We were both covered in snow and I was just going to ask what he was up to when suddenly he spoke: 'Good morning, PC Johnson, how are you enjoying this weather?'

I couldn't believe my ears or eyes. To see a sergeant out in this weather was okay, to see an inspector very doubtful, but to see Superintendent Rowe, the head of the whole division, was something else. I tried to salute him but my cape was heavy with snow and all I succeeded in doing was to cover him with more snow, but luckily for me he just laughed.

Because we had pre-designated routes to follow he knew where I was supposed to be and so he came and found me.

'I'm just checking that all my men are safe and okay. If they have to work in this terrible snow then so should I. Come on, we'll walk back to the station together. I know that you've checked all your properties because I followed your footsteps in the snow.'

By the end of the night shift the super had spent about an hour with each of us working the beat in the thick snow. I remembered the words that PC Roy Sharman had used on my very first shift: 'Just remember – if you earn respect, you'll get it back.' The super had done just that with us mere mortals that night and none of us ever forgot it.

The night shift was always my favourite shift down The Cliffe, as there was far less traffic and fewer people knocking about. Attercliffe was like a city within a city and when I arrived there in 1962, aged just nineteen, I wondered what had hit me.

I'd left the small rural pit village of Darfield behind me and started work in the busiest part of one of the biggest cities in England. Sheffield was also the most important place in the world for the manufacture of steel and cutlery; and to facilitate this, tens of thousands of people worked in and around Attercliffe, often on a three-shift system. For this reason The Cliffe was never quiet and in those days, if someone had placed a blindfold across my eyes I would always know when I was down The Cliffe because of the distinctive noises and smells given off during the steel manufacturing processes. Both were awesome and, after a while, you got used to the noise and the fact that your mouth was often clogged up with dust whilst walking the beat.

The upside to all this, however, was the fact that the east end of Sheffield was a fantastic and vibrant place to work. It was full of characters, some bad, but in the main good, honest friendly and hard-working people, just as I like them. I made long-lasting friendships with people of many different nationalities and I learned something new from each and every one of them over the years.

The winter weather conditions of 1962–3 seemed to last for ever, and there was even packed ice on the pavements at the Manor Top well into May. Eventually the weather improved and, when it got warmer, it was as if the city had come back to life; people were smiling again and looked more relaxed.

Saturday nights, on both afters (3pm to 11pm) and nights (11pm to 7am), were always busy in Attercliffe and Darnall. About half of the workforce were on a night off and intended to give the ball a good kick, and enjoy themselves.

On this particular occasion I was on foot patrol at Darnall

and working from 3pm to 11pm – supposedly. When all the pubs turned out there was often some sort of bother and it was rare to finish on time.

At about 4.30pm I was standing on Darnall Terminus watching the comings and goings. People were shopping for the weekend and various bakers, greengrocers and butchers were all very busy. I glanced down the road towards Child's, the chemist, and noticed a lad of about twenty anxiously pacing up and down outside the shop. He was wearing a dark suit with drainpipe trousers, complete with suede shoes with thick crepe soles. His Brylcreemed quiff shone in the sunlight. He was obviously a rocker or teddy boy, but what was he doing?

After a few more minutes of pacing, he dashed into the chemist's and then two minutes later he came out again and continued his pacing. I was intrigued and moved nearer to the chemist's shop to observe him more closely. After about ten minutes and more pacing he dashed back into the shop and then a couple of minutes later he was out again and pacing up and down. I moved closer to the shop but kept out of sight. Every time he came out of the shop he had his hand in his inside jacket pocket and whatever his game was, he was mine.

Shoplifting? But what would he steal from a chemist's shop? No, he was about to rob the shop; it was nearing closing time and the till would be full. It must either be a knife or a gun inside his jacket, so I'd have to be mindful of that.

At this point he dashed into the shop again and I ran across the road and into the passageway at the side of the shop. A couple of minutes later, he came out with his hand in his pocket again and I pulled him into the passageway before he could do anything. Grabbing the arm that was in his jacket, I pulled it out and got the shock of my life: no gun, no knife but a brand-new, still in its box, toothbrush! What the hell? I checked his inside pocket and recovered three more toothbrushes and three combs in plastic cases.

'Why would you steal three combs and four toothbrushes?' I asked.

'I haven't stolen them. I've bought them, even though I didn't want them.'

'You must be joking. Why?' I asked again.

'I'm going out with the lads tonight to the Lacarno Ballroom,' he replied.

'What's that got to do with combs and toothbrushes?'

'I was hoping to pull a bird and have a bit of – you know. A bit of mankin [sex].'

'Just what the hell are you talking about?'

'I went to the chemist's to buy some johnnies [condoms] but the girls in the shop know mi mum.'

'What's that got to do with combs and toothbrushes?' I asked yet again, exasperatedly.

'When I got to the counter and the lady asked me what I wanted, I went all embarrassed like and panicked in case she told mi mum, so every time I went into the shop I panicked again and bought a comb or toothbrush instead.'

I couldn't believe what I was hearing and couldn't stop laughing.

I could see that he was telling the truth and I must have scared him to death, poor lad. In those days there was no pill and a packet of three condoms (3s 9d, about 19 pence in modern money) was the only protection available. I had to somehow make amends. I explained to the lad, who was called Gary, what I had witnessed and reacted to and he said that he'd have thought the same as me, thank goodness. 'Wait there, Gary. I'll be back in a minute,' I said.

Knowing the girls in the shop, I walked to the counter and was met by Sylvia the manageress. 'Yes Constable, we're just closing, what can I get you?'

Back outside, Gary was waiting in the passageway and, judging from the eager look on his face, he'd worked out what I was up to.

'Well?' he asked.

'Here you are,' and I passed him a pack of three. 'Have them on me, pal – good luck.'

'Thanks but don't tell mi mum, will you – I've never been with a girl so far.' I was laughing all the way back to the nick and when I told the lads at snap time they did the same.

I used to bump into him about every couple of weeks or so and I nicknamed him 'Gossamer Gary'. Every time I saw him the first question was always the same: 'Any luck, Gary?'

'No, I'm no good at chatting 'em up, even mi mum wants to know why I haven't got a bird.'

Some time after this I was walking down Staniforth Road when I saw Gossamer Gary across the road, but he was walking with the help of two crutches. I crossed the road to talk to him and, when he saw me, his face was all smiles.

'What's tha up to nah?' I asked.

'I met this girl at bingo in t' Aqueduct Club and took her home last week.'

'But why are you on crutches?'

'I'd just used the last of them Durex you got me – it were about two o'clock in t' morning and I came out o' t' house an' I was so happy and excited that I did a cartwheel on t' pavement. It were dark an' a din't see t' bleedin' gas lamp; and I hit it an' broke my leg an' three ribs, but it were worth it – she's gorgeous.'

'You barmy pillock, but congratulations.' What a boy, and once again I was hysterical with laughing.

'Can you get me some more johnnies? I still daren't get 'em.'

'You're a man now, pal and if you're going mankin get your own!' Eighteen months later I was invited to the wedding of Gary and a lovely girl called Ann, and guess what I took as a wedding present? Yes, you're half right, I took a packet of Durex and a canteen of cutlery, which, because Sheffield was the cutlery capital of the world in those days, was quite cheap and I got them direct from the manufacturer. Gary went to work at the steelworks in Port Talbot in Wales and I often think about him and his wife. I hope they are okay now. In those days there were no vending machines selling Durex in gents' toilets. If he still daren't get them from the chemist's shop, he could well have twenty mouths to feed by now. I'd love to meet up with him again and chat about old times and see how he's going on.

A few days after nearly arresting Gossamer Gary for armed robbery of a comb and toothbrush, I was walking down Main Road when a chap pulled up in his car and told me that a Tenant's Brewery lorry had hit the side of the aqueduct bridge further down Darnall Main Road.

At this point the canal was carried by an aqueduct over the road and the road itself dipped down under the bridge. The road was quite narrow here and as I neared the scene the smell of beer was getting stronger. I could see that the lorry had caught the side of the bridge and its entire load of wooden beer barrels had fallen on to the road and smashed open on impact.

It was the school holidays and there were dozens of kids of

all ages watching the proceedings. They and their pet dogs were seeing something different. It was a poor area of Sheffield and, because no one was hurt, I was able to enjoy a chat and a laugh along with them. It wasn't a busy road but I had to close it, there were broken barrels everywhere.

Whilst waiting for the City Cleansing Department to come and remove the debris, I noticed more kids and dogs arriving and also mums and dads. I knew a lot of them and we were all chatting and having a laugh.

There seemed to be a lot of loud laughter at the opposite side of the bridge to where I was, so being nosy I went to look and find out why. On the pavement near to a small crowd was a black-and-white Jack Russell dog. It was in a sitting position with its head pointing skywards and howling loudly. At first I thought the poor thing was injured but then, looking down into the hollow under the bridge, I could see the cause of all the laughter.

It was a red-hot summer's day and, like me, the dogs were thirsty. Labradors, greyhounds, whippets, alsatians and poodles were all enjoying a free beer. They were literally lapping it up. First one and then another were howling their heads off and some were falling over just like drunken men, and every time they tried to regain their feet they were falling all over the place. More and more people must have heard what was happening and came to watch the goings on. There must have been 150 people there watching the funny antics of about twenty dogs in varying stages of drunkenness and one or two of them had to be carried home by their owners. What a sight! I can honestly say that it has to rank as one of the three funniest things I have ever witnessed. At that point the Cleansing Department arrived and cleared the barrels, which allowed the road to be opened once more, thus spoiling all our fun and that of the dogs. It is something I'll never forget.

Whippet and greyhound racing were major sports in and around Sheffield in those days and a few days later I talked to Alan, the owner of one of the greyhounds that was more than a bit tipsy.

'How's the dog, mate?' I asked.

'He's only just coming round. He slept for three days solid. I reckon he supped more ale that day than even I can cope with,' he replied laughingly.

'Will he be able to race again?' I asked.

'Race again? You're joking; he can't even stand up yet.' He then went on to say, 'I reckon that if I replace the hare with a pint of that beer he'd win his next race easy trying to get at it.'

CHAPTER THREE

Men of Steel

The day shift (7am to 3pm) down The Cliffe was usually fairly routine. There was light rain falling, so I wore my cape as I walked the couple of miles from my lodgings to the main 'nick' at Whitworth Lane, Attercliffe.

I arrived at about 6.50am having walked past Brown Bayley's steelworks, the one with the loud and large drop hammer. The pollution in Attercliffe was amazing and all the buildings, including the austere-looking Victorian nick, were blackened with soot. The Cliffe was never quiet and even at this time of day the place was teeming with people going to work. Very few bobbies could afford cars then, including me, and buses or shanks's pony (walking) were the main modes of transport.

After I'd signed on and had a chat with the lads we all

went out on our respective beats. At 8.30am the kids from Maltby Street School started to arrive. They were all running because of the rain, so I took them across from one side of Attercliffe Common to the other as quickly as I could. One poor lad looked in a sorry state. He had a plaster covering the left-hand lens of his glasses (to combat a lazy eye) and purple dye on his head (to combat ringworm). He had a lovely smile on his face, which got even bigger when I gave him some barley-sugar sweets from my pocket. I loved taking the kids across the road at school times; they were all so different and by 9.05am it was all over, even the poor ragtags, with no coats to keep them dry, had run faster than normal to miss the rain.

Today was the day to deliver the pawnbrokers' notices to all the swap shops and scrap-metal dealers in the area. These notices listed details and descriptions of property stolen in the area over the last couple of weeks, including, of course, metal. In those days Sheffield was the metal capital of the world and the theft of steel, lead, copper, brass and aluminium was big business. Large thefts of metal from all over the country would often end up in Sheffield, having been bought by unsuspecting scrap dealers (don't laugh). There were scrapyards all over the city but mainly down The Cliffe, this being central to where the melting furnaces were located.

All the scrap lads were characters and there was a form of

hierarchy. First in line were the lads who went round all the 'deries' (derelict houses), chopping out the lead piping and copper wire from within the empty houses. This was usually sold on to the rag-and-bone men with their horse and carts, who walked or rode on their carts shouting, 'Any old iron, rag, bone, any old iron, rag, bone.' A few shillings (there were twenty in a pound) would change hands and that's how the rag-and-bone man made his living. The ragman would then save all the small bits of scrap he bought until he had enough for a decent 'weigh-in' at one of the small scrap-yards, which were numerous and the next rung up in the hierarchy.

These lads, who were always ducking and diving to avoid getting caught with bent gear, had yards where they had piles of car batteries, car radiators, copper wire and aluminium. All of this was non-ferrous metal which wouldn't 'take the magnet' and was worth a lot more than the ferrous scrap (iron) which also needed a lot of space to store.

The lads then sold it on to the big men in the scrap game who had massive yards full of piles of scrap cars, ferrous metals of different types along with iron girders. The iron girders were moved from and to different parts of the yard by overhead cranes with massive magnets hanging beneath them with which to offload the wagons that brought iron to the yard. The metal was cut up with acetylene torches and stacked for shipment to various melting shops in the area.

This made the identification of stolen scrap very difficult and was the reason for our visits to the scrapyards. Details of the type of scrap, and the form that it was in, was described on the notices. This meant that if a scrap dealer was caught in possession of the same, after having been informed of its theft, he then had some explaining to do. If the truth was ever told, I'm sure that most of the notices ended up on a nail at the back of the toilet door with all the other squares of newspaper used for bum fodder.

Talking of bum fodder, all the back-to-back and off-shot houses had outside toilets in those days, which was handy for us when working the beat on night shift. We were spoiled for choice if we were taken short!

A scrap dealer's transport could vary greatly. The local knife-and-scissor grinder, for example, used a push-bike similar to our police bikes but with a small grindstone which, when attached to a belt and pulley, could be turned by pedalling when the bike was on a stand. He would sharpen householders' knives and scissors and, perhaps, buy old cutlery for scrap in return for a few pence.

The likely lads who raided the empty houses used a wheelbarrow and the ragman used his horse and cart. These were followed by the bigger likely lads with small yards and big weighing scales. They usually drove a small pick-up truck that would be lucky to pass its MOT and these lads would also have access to a van. If they drove past you in a van as opposed to a pick-up you were less likely to pull them over and search the vehicle for stolen metal.

If you were at the top of the tree or a 'big mester', you usually drove a Roller or Bentley and wore a Reed and Taylor suit made by Barnie Goodman – the best money could buy. The big mesters had not been born into money, nor had they gone to fancy schools, they were belt-and-braces men who had worked hard to get where they were and they weren't afraid to get their hands mucky. What some, but by no means all, lacked in academic qualifications was more than made up for through hard graft, a nose for a deal and the experiences gained whilst making their way up to the top of the ladder. A huge percentage of people in Sheffield and surrounding towns depended on steel and other metals. The city steelworks needed the expertise of the scrap men to make sure they got all the metals that were required and some of the scrap lads, in turn, ensured that they could supply those needs by whatever means available – nudge, nudge, wink, wink.

In 1961 the famous E-Type Jaguar came out and in January 1963 the new vehicles registration system was introduced. For the first time vehicles were given a letter at the end of the usual registration mark (eg ABC 123A). These letters became a recognisable status symbol and some of the first ones to be seen were on vehicles owned by the big boys of the scrap game. They'd worked hard for what they'd got and wanted to show it off – good luck to them.

From these large scrapyards lorry-loads of different types of metal were delivered to the various melting shops and furnaces around the city such as British Steel, where metal could be melted down and recycled into ingots. From there these ingots and metal bars would be delivered to the many Sheffield forgemasters who would rework the metal into the different shapes required in the manufacturing process.

As well as scrap-metal dealers, we also delivered notices to pawnbrokers' 'uncles' as they were known then. If anything had to be pawned by poor families, they would tell the kids that they had taken whatever the goods were (usually a gold watch or chain or something similar) to 'uncle' for him to look after.

At that time there was only one pawnbroker in the Attercliffe Division, as most had been replaced by 'swap shops' and second-hand dealers.

Swap shops or 'pop shops' played a similar role to pawnbrokers and there were quite a few in our Division. The two nearest the nick were both on Attercliffe Common; one at the end of Whitworth Lane and the other at the top of Leigh Street.

Both shops sold second-hand and new goods as well. I'd never seen shops like these before and I found them fascinating. They sold radios, musical instruments, tools, fishing tackle, watches and all manner of things. In those days

Green Shield Stamps were given away at petrol stations and I think you got one for every gallon of petrol you bought. A pound would buy you three gallons; a lot different from today's prices. If you saved the stamps up you could redeem them for goods only, but if you wanted cash, then the swap shops would buy the books of stamps off you. The same applied to cigarette coupons like Kensitas and No. 6 brands.

As I walked down Attercliffe Common towards Tinsley, it was still raining and my cape felt heavy. I needed to scrounge a cuppa somewhere and get out of the rain, and knew just the place. Just past Carbrook School and before you got to Broughton Lane was Gallons' Grocer's shop. Painted on the shop window in white distemper were the prices for some of the goods which were for sale inside. The shop was run by a lovely couple in their mid-forties, Eddie and Alice Boyles, and they had a son called Michael, who was a similar age to me. Eddie and Alice wore long white coats and, as we were chatting over a mug of tea, I watched them weighing out sugar, which they put into blue paper bags ready for sale. They did the same with flour and coconut which had been delivered to the premises in enormous hessian sacks. Inside the display counter were large round cheeses, waiting to be cut and weighed according to the customers' requirements, along with a massive block of real butter. The smell of fresh coffee beans (also in sacks) and the fresh leaf tea, which came in wooden chests like the ones we used for skiffle groups as youngsters, made the shop smell lovely and homely.

The shop was situated in a poor working-class area and some of the women who came to shop would only order what they could afford.

'Can you weigh me two ounces of butter, Alice? And can I have three rashers of thin bacon and two ounces of mucky drippin' for t' kids' tea?' While Eddie was slicing the rashers of bacon on the deep red Ascot bacon machine, the conversation continued.

'Can I pay for it on Friday, Eddie, when Harry gets paid please?'

'Alright Florence, you always pay on time, I'll write it in the 'Tick' book,' replied Eddie.

'Thanks duck, I'll have two eggs as well now you've said that. That coffee smells good but we can only drink it when we visit me mam – God bless you both and thank you.' And off she went.

'If we didn't let 'em run a slate up some of them would starve,' said Eddie, 'but very rarely do they let us down.'

I thanked them for the cuppa and after leaving the lovely smells behind I made my way down The Common and past the Broughton Inn. Every time I got to Clifton Street, situated just past Broughton Lane, I always had two separate lots of laughs. Glancing to my right I could see the reason for the first laugh. Behind Wraggs' timber merchants was, of all things, in the middle of the heavy industry, a business selling boats. The nearest river was the Don, but this wasn't navigable because of the several weirs, and the nearest sea was the North Sea, about seventy miles away. The people who owned it were great and made a good living, but its geographical position tickled me pink and made me laugh.

As I have said, when I joined the force in 1962 I was only just nineteen, very naive and had no idea about city life. Luckily for me I was working amongst the finest coppers in the land and they looked after me and showed me the ropes.

Most bobbies smoked in those days, including me and I'd noticed that some of the lads who I looked up to and respected the most smoked a pipe; people like Roy Sharman, Les Newsome, Jeff Loukes and Frank Lyndsey who were all 'proper mesters' in my book.

To me, at nineteen, they looked the part and, wanting to be like them, I also bought a pipe. The stem was made of aluminium and I think it was called a Falcon. It nearly killed me, I was inhaling like I did with a fag, but I persevered and couldn't wait for the night shift so that I could smoke it whilst walking the beat, just like them.

Apart from burning my finger trying to tamp down the hot 'baccy' in the pipe bowl, I felt like one of the lads, and all was going well until I got to Clifton Street. I'd 'shaken hands' with all the shop-door handles down The Common, checking for break-ins and was doing the same in Clifton Street. Clifton Street was pitch black apart from the odd dimly lit gas lamp; and I had my police-issue metal lamp in my right hand and the pipe between my teeth. I checked the boatyard and the Methodist chapel, where Eddie from Gallons' played the organ, and Michael ran the youth club; and thought I heard a noise further down the cobbled street, near to a small shop. At 2am it had to be someone up to no good. I stopped and listened for a minute, but nothing. The noise had sounded muffled but like breaking glass. I slowly crept forward with nerves jangling, but when I stopped again and waited I still heard nothing. I slowly crept up the passageway between the house and the shop thinking that I must have been hearing things. The lamp batteries were running out and I could hardly see a bloody thing. By the time I got to the top of the passageway, my heart was beating faster and I felt like a coiled spring.

I could hear shallow breathing nearby but couldn't see anything. Whoosh, bang, I was pushed or thrown against the wall by someone who was now legging it down the passage. Spinning round to chase him and with my heart nearly jumping out of my chest two things happened at once. I'd bumped into something and there was the biggest clang I'd ever heard; I'll bet they heard it in Scotland Yard, it was that loud. Then I tripped, fell over and there was another almighty clang. My face and mouth were hurting like hell and I didn't know what was happening.

As the lamp flickered back to life I could see a large zinc bath in the middle of the passageway and I realized that I must have knocked it from its hanging place on the wall at one side of the passageway and, at the same time, tripped over it. I could smell burning, which wasn't surprising. I'd hit the bath, still with the f —— pipe in my mouth and the bowl was now under my nose. It was still alight, which was a miracle in itself as I had been trying all night to keep the damned thing lit, and it was burning the end of my nose and scorching the hairs up it. The stem had jammed into the back of my throat and it felt like it was sticking out of the back of my neck. I must have looked like Popeye.

My eyes were stinging and watering and the pain in my mouth was really bad. I could vaguely make out bedroom lights coming on in the street and sash windows opening. The noise made from the zinc bath falling on the floor must have woken up everyone in The Cliffe.

'What the bloody hell's going on now?' somebody shouted, 'Do you know what bloody time it is? We've got to go to work tomorrow. Clear off.' I checked the rear of the shop and found some broken glass which had been removed from one of the windows, but luckily for the shopkeeper I must have disturbed the would-be burglar before he could steal anything. I could barely talk, but eventually told the neighbours that all was well and that they could go back to bed.

Unfortunately I never caught the culprit, but if I had I would have made him eat milk pobs (small milk-soaked portions of bread) for a week just as I had to.

On the way back to the nick I was thinking that if smoking a pipe made me like one of the lads then I didn't want to know, so as I walked up Tinsley Park Road on my way back to the nick I threw the f —— pipe into the canal, which is where my pink-and-yellow bike had ended up a few weeks earlier (see Chapter 7 in *What's Tha Up To?* for this story in full).

I've never smoked a pipe from that day to this, they're too dangerous and now I stick to fags.

At the time it was far from funny, I was in agony for a week but now, even today when I drive up The Common and see Clifton Street, I burst out laughing.

CHAPTER FOUR

A Policeman's Lot is Not Always a Happy One

Being a beat bobby was, to me, something very special. It gave me the opportunity to meet and talk to people from all walks of life and reminded me of the song from *The King and I*, 'Getting to Know You'.

My favourite people were kids and old people. To me it was a thrill to walk the beat and hear a child shout from across the road, 'PC Johnson!' and then follow it with a wave and a smile. I would always return the smile and the wave and their little chests would puff out with pride, especially if they were with their mum and dad.

In between duties I would pass the time of day with as many people as possible, and I loved it.

A lot of old people are lonely and have no one to talk to, and the secret with them is to listen. Most had survived the Second World War and had stories to tell like, 'Did I ever tell you about when I was at the Battle of El Alamein?'

'I don't think so, but I'd love to hear it,' I'd reply.

The ladies told different stories to the men: 'When I was in service' or 'I was in the munitions factory in the war making bullets for our troops, you know.'

I've always respected older people, as without them we wouldn't be here, so even though I'd heard the same stories, often from the same people, I adopted one rule: LISTEN. They were quite rightly proud of what they'd done and been through and had earned the right to be listened to and treated with respect and I loved them all. In my opinion too many people suffer from 'I' disease (I this, I that or I the other) and we should all learn to listen more and allow someone to be happier for us having done so.

I applied the same rule to criminals. I'll never forget a detective sergeant telling a young PC mate of mine called John Morgan not to talk to criminals – what a load of old b —— . Just like the old people, I've talked to loads of them, either in the street or over a beer, and it is surprising what they tell you. Some, after a few beers, are daft enough to brag about their latest 'job' and most have an enemy or two in the criminal fraternity who they grass on; and I've felt many a criminal's collar just because I've listened. Young John did the same as me and listened, which was good because he retired as a gaffer – good for him. He was a good lad and when he first joined the job he was in the same digs as me at Mrs Proctor's on Elmham Road, Darnall, where we had many a good laugh together.

Those of you who have read my first book *What's Tha Up To?* will know what I mean when I say that when working the beat absolutely anything can happen and often does. The nature of the job means that you have to expect the unexpected and, in those days, you were on your own. No mobile phones, no walkie-talkies, just the public telephone kiosk to keep you in touch with the main nick, or the police box of which there were only six in the whole division: at Hartley Brook Road (First Park), Earl Marshal Road (Grimesthorpe), Sheffield Road (Tinsley), Attercliffe Road and Staniforth Road/Handsworth Road and Woodthorpe on the Manor Estate. There were also tiny sub-stations at Firth Park, Darnall, Manor Top and Woodhouse, with one to three officers working the beat from them. It was a huge area to cover, with a population of about 250,000.

For our own safety we were required to work a pre-designated route given to the office sergeant. He knew, in theory, where to find us, and every twenty minutes we had to be at a different geographical point on the beat. This was usually where there was a telephone kiosk, and this was the only way that we could communicate with the divisional office or them with us.

Before the days of lollipop men/ladies we used to work school crossing duties on the major routes and on this particular day I had taken the kids from Whitby Road School across Staniforth Road when they finished at 3.30pm.

The sun was shining and it was very hot, just as it had been for the past week or two, and for this reason we were allowed to work in shirtsleeve order, with our sleeves rolled up and our pocketbook and whistle in our shirt pockets. I had a quick cuppa at the petrol station opposite Bone Cravens Engineering's workshops where security was very tight as they were fitting out a very special railway carriage for the Shah of Persia and a lot of the fittings were made of gold.

After a chat with Stan, the petrol station owner, and Mabel Wright, the pump attendant (no self-service then), I set off down Staniforth Road. I'd arranged to call in and see Mabel and her husband Roy later that evening, as they had kindly asked me to be godfather to Alan, their baby son. What a compliment.

As I got to the telephone kiosk at the top of Garth Road I could hear the phone ringing so I answered it. At the other end was Sergeant Dennis Hoyland, a tough old boy but a good and well-respected man. He told me that someone had rung the station reporting the smell of gas a few streets from where I was and would I investigate.

As I walked past the house in Nidd Road, where the motor-bike accident had happened a few months ago (see Chapter 14 in *What's Tha Up To?*), I couldn't help laughing to myself and wondering how Mary and Albert were going on.

On my arrival at the house, which was next to the end house in a long row of terraced houses where the complaint of a smell of gas came from, I knocked on the door. The door opened to reveal a fairly young couple who had both recently arrived home from work. The smell hit me and I instantly knew what it was.

'I can assure you both that it's not gas,' I said. 'When did you first notice it?'

'A few weeks ago, I think,' replied the man.

'Has it got any stronger since then?' I asked.

'Funnily enough, yes, which is why I've rung you, but with it being hot we leave doors and windows open to let the fresh air in,' he answered.

'Have you asked the people next door if they can smell it?' I asked.

'No, we're new here and haven't met the neighbours yet. The ones that way' (he pointed to his right) 'are away, I think and the ones on the left are an oldish couple.'

'I'll just check with the neighbours and I'll be back in a bit,' I said.

I was glad to leave the house as I knew, from experience, what the smell was and I didn't want to alarm them. Knocking on the door of the house next door produced a minor surprise for me. Standing in the open doorway was a lady of about seventy-five, dressed in a full-length pinafore. It was one of the old ladies I often spoke to when she was shopping on Darnall Terminus, but today she looked a hundred years old. 'Do you mind if I come into the house?' I gently asked, and she agreed. I took a big gasp of air and went in, whilst trying desperately not to be sick. The stench was incredible – the stench of death.

The old lady seemed to be in a trance as I glanced round the house and I knew that I needed to handle this situation with great care and tact.

'Where's your husband, love?' I asked.

'Alf's a lovely man but he hasn't been very well, duck.'

'Perhaps I can have a chat with him. Maybe cheer him up a bit.'

'I'm sorry, duck, but he's fast asleep.'

'I'll just have a little look at him, love. Don't worry, it'll be okay. Is he upstairs?'

'Yes, but don't wake him up, he's so tired.'

'Okay love, I've put you the kettle on, you mash a cuppa tea and I'll not be long.'

Out of sight of the old lady, I covered my nose with a handkerchief and breathed in and out through my mouth only, which kept the revolting smell away from my nostrils to some degree. I climbed the stairs very slowly, swatting at a large amount of bluebottle flies at the same time.

Poor old Alf was in the room nearest to the young couple's bedroom next door and the smell must have percolated through the cracks in the ceiling and walls. The room was red hot and I opened the sash window, noticing at the same time a small electric fire near to the bottom of the bed, which was switched on. Judging by the neighbours' comments, I realised that Alf must have been dead for some time and, because he was cold, she must have tried to keep him warm, poor lass.

Alf was in bed and covered up to his chin in bedclothes and he was badly decomposed. On top of the bedclothes near to his chin was a dinner plate and a spoon. The plate contained the rotted remains of a meal, parts of which were also on the bedclothes, and what I saw next shook me rigid. When I looked at him more closely I could see that his mouth was stuffed full of rotted food and I realised that the poor old lady had been trying to feed him after he was dead. What must she have gone through? I could have wept for her.

Back downstairs she was sitting in the kitchen, so I made her a cup of strong tea with sugar and then I opened the window to let some air in. 'Is he still asleep? I hope you've not woke him up,' she said. 'He doesn't eat much, you know,

48

and that's why he's tired.' I'm not often stuck for words but I was then; my heart went out to her and I just wanted to put my arms around her.

A lovely day had just turned into a lousy one and it was difficult to work out what to do next. The old lady had cracked up and I had to ascertain death officially, even though it was obvious, and then I had to get the body to the mortuary. As far as I was concerned the old lady's welfare was my priority; the dead body could wait.

I told her that I was nipping to the Co-op shop at the end of the road and that I'd be back in a minute or two. Leaving my helmet in the house I ran to the shop, being mindful of leaving the lady on her own. I quickly outlined the situation to the manager, whom I knew, and asked him to telephone for the local doctor, enquiring at the same time if the old lady had any local friends or relatives. He obliged in both directions. He sent for the doctor and a lady from round the corner who knew the old lady reasonably well. Before the lady and I left to go back to the house, I explained to her about the smell, to which she replied, 'I haven't seen Ethel knocking about for a few weeks and now I know why. Don't worry about the smell, duck. I lay bodies out for an undertaker. Shall I bring my laying-out board and pennies to keep his eyes shut?'

'Not today, love. Unless the doctor gives the cause of death, he'll have to go to the mortuary,' I replied.

49

'If that happens, I'll take Ethel to my house and get our Bill to fetch her sister, who lives in Rotherham. She doesn't visit often because she can't climb onto the bus,' she said.

'That's very kind of you, and thanks for helping out,' I said.

'That's what neighbours are for, love,' she replied.

A few minutes after our arrival back at the house, the local doctor arrived and gave Ethel a sedative to settle her down a bit. Upstairs he certified the death but, because of the state of the body, he could not issue a certificate as to the cause of death, so there would have to be a post-mortem.

At my request the doctor phoned the police station from his surgery nearby and related the story, at the same time asking for the mortuary van to attend so that we could remove the body – a job I wasn't looking forward to, to say the least.

The neighbour took Ethel to her home when the van arrived, which left the driver and me to get on with the job. Luckily he had some rubber gloves in the van and a large rubber sheet. As we tried to move the body onto the rubber sheet it just gently collapsed and fell apart. What a mess – maggots and all. Why did I join the bloody police force? We took the body to the mortuary in Nursery Street and, because there were no signs of suspicious circumstances, I wrote a report and went back to my digs. That was one of the messiest dead bodies I ever dealt with and even the doctor had been sick. I stank like a midden and obviously could not go back into my digs. Mrs Proctor, my landlady, passed me some new clothes and I burned my uniform shirt, trousers and underclothes in the back garden. It took me days, several baths and much nail-cleaning before I was able to pick up a sandwich again. I just didn't feel clean enough to do so and you never forget a smell like that.

Just over a week later I caught the 71 bus to Manor Top and then walked down City Road to the cemetery. Even though it was my day off I was in uniform and, as the hearse containing Alf drew near, I put on my white gloves, stood to attention and saluted the coffin, just as we always did in those days.

Dealing with sudden deaths was all part of the job and you become hardened to most of them, but some are sadder than others and you don't forget them. Alf had died of a heart attack and Ethel didn't want to lose him. In her own mind she had convinced herself that he was still alive, and thought she was doing the right thing by feeding him and keeping him warm. It was a first for me and all the other lads that I spoke to.

After the council cleaned and fumigated the house, Ethel moved back in. A few weeks later I was on nights and called into Enos Kays, the flower and vegetable wholesalers in the Parkway wholesale market. I spoke to Alan, the manager, told him the story and he gave me a few flowers which I took to Ethel. She was glad to see me and thanked me for going to the funeral. She seemed okay, but was obviously missing Alf.

One day in mid-January, a few months after Alf's death, I bumped into Ethel's neighbour on Darnall Terminus and I asked her how Ethel was doing.

'Didn't you know?' she replied.

'Know what?' I asked.

'She committed suicide with tablets on Christmas Day and left a note saying that she wanted to be with Alf again.'

What a tragedy. Loneliness can sometimes be an illness and as serious as cancer in circumstances like that, which is why even to this day I talk and listen to as many older people as I can. It's all too easy to allow someone to become a stranger and they think that no one cares any more. So if you are reading this, just pause a bit and think of the people you know who may just need to talk. Good luck and well done.

Anyway, enough of death, let's move on.

CHAPTER FIVE

Lessons Learned the Hard Way

'Johnson, the morning inspector wants to see you. Knock on his door and when he tells you to come in, walk to his desk, stand to attention and salute him. Okay?'

'Yes, Sergeant,' I replied.

Only having been on the job for three months I was worried sick. What did he want? I'd just finished a quiet night shift at 7am. My mind was racing; I must be in bother for something, but what? And then it dawned on me and my heart sank – he must somehow know.

My designated snap time had been 2.30am and after my potted-meat sandwich and a banana, I was back on the beat at 3.15am. I was working the main Attercliffe Road area which stretched almost all the way from Sheffield to Rotherham, and on either side of the road were a couple of hundred shops to check for break-ins. As a result of this, I worked on one side of the road and another bobby worked the other, and if the sergeant caught you having a chat to each other you were in the s — t.

At about 5am I'd bumped into PC Terry Bruce, who shouted me to join him across the road and look at something. He was standing outside a shop that sold babywear and prams, and he'd found, at the back of the premises, an old display model of a stork, the ones that people told their kids delivered babies in their beaks. It had obviously been put out as rubbish.

'Come on,' said Terry, 'we'll have some fun with this,' and he promptly placed it in the middle of the road that took traffic travelling from Sheffield to Rotherham. In those days there was far less traffic than there is today, especially at five in the morning. We crept into the dark alley between the shops and waited to see what would happen.

It was about ten minutes before we saw a car approaching us in the distance. What would the driver make of it? Headlights on, he started to slow down when he saw the dummy stork. I could see it better now, and at three-and-a-half-feet tall it looked like the real thing. The car slowed down to fifteen miles per hour and then gently swerved round it and drove on. Me and Terry looked at each other and laughed but, to be honest, didn't think it all that funny.

After about ten minutes another car came into view and

we couldn't believe what happened next. The car, a big oldish Austin, slowly pulled up and stopped about forty feet from the bird; you could see the driver stretching his neck closer to the windscreen to get a better look and we couldn't stop laughing. At that point the driver slowly and quietly opened his car door, got out and peered at the stork over the top of his door. Of course, it was made of papier mâché and obviously didn't move and so the driver, a middle-aged chap in what appeared to be a dark suit, walked slowly towards it and, with his arms and fingers outstretched towards our bird, shouted, 'Shoo! Shoo! Shoo!' whilst waving his arms about. The man then got back into his car and drove away towards Rotherham. Terry and I were almost hysterical, and we were laughing that much that we didn't see the large post-office lorry coming down the road. He didn't even slow down and smashed our poor stork into a thousand little pieces, stopping any future fun.

It was good to have a laugh while working, in view of what you normally have to deal with; things like accidents, fights, deaths and so on, but now it seemed that I was going to pay the price for having a bit of fun. I knocked on the inspector's door. 'Come in,' he shouted. I braced myself for what was coming next as I marched to the front of his desk and saluted.

'Ah, PC Johnson, I'm sending you to London.'

'I beg your pardon, sir?'

'Here's your railway ticket. I'll get someone to take you to the station. The train leaves in half an hour.' I couldn't believe or understand what he was on about and I was ready for a kip but daren't say. Luckily, he continued, 'Right, put your civvy jacket on, catch the train to London and then get a taxi to the DPP's office in the Strand. Deliver this box (pointing to a container on his desk) and then return in your own time. Okay?'

'Sir, what does DPP mean?' I daren't ask about getting some shut-eye.

'Director of Public Prosecution's offices and in that box there are highly important documents relating to a major court case. I know it's your day off, so get a sandwich on the train and get some sleep; you look tired.' With that, he gave me two £5 notes (a lot of money in those days) and off he went, chuckling to himself which I thought was odd.

Once on the train I started to think. If someone had given me a million guesses as to why the Inspector wanted to see me, I would never have got it right. I couldn't believe I was going to London of all places and I was hoping the taxi man would know where I had to go. Today it's nothing I know, but fifty years ago it was a major event for a lad of nineteen from a pit village to visit the great metropolis.

I'd been to London once before on a trip from Darfield School and I didn't like it. It was too busy for me as a ten-year-old. I remember going to Battersea Power Station and

Billingsgate Fish Market, but I've no idea why. My good friend from the age of four, Roy Williamson, and I were that tired when we got to Westminster Abbey that we fell asleep on a pew. Roy was easily the cleverest boy in the class, and must have been impressed with the power station because he ended up being the boss of several generating stations throughout the country over the years.

Eventually I arrived and got a taxi to the DPP's office, depositing the box in return for a receipt. Now I was a bit more relaxed and walked the short distance to Trafalgar Square and marvelled at the number of people I saw coming and going. Apart from the mums and dads with their kids who were feeding the birds, I didn't see anyone smile or talk to each other. I watched the feral or wild pigeons and all I could think of was a big fat wood pigeon. Sliced wood pigeon breast, bacon, black pudding and mushy peas were, to me, a meal fit for a king.

I'd had enough after half an hour and decided to get back to the station. I had to laugh to myself: a few hours ago I was laughing like crazy watching how a man dealt with a dummy stork in the very grimy East End of Sheffield and now here I was in London, the capital of England, and the world for that matter, in those days.

I felt like a mole on the tube, down one hole and then up another, people packed like sardines and if you smiled at them they looked at you in amazement. I remember thinking at the time, let me get out of here and back to normality.

Eventually, and after a few mishaps on the tube, I got back to the station only to find that I'd got about an hour to wait for the next train home. I found the station café, bought some food, fags and a paper and sat at a table near the door where I could watch the goings-on. The food wasn't good but the tea in a mug was grand, especially with a fag.

Just after this I think I must have nodded off because I woke up with a jolt. The café had got busier and I'd been joined at the table by three foreign chaps who also had a mug of tea each. I couldn't tell a word they were saying, but smiled and got a fag from the packet which I'd left on the table. The next thing I knew was that all three of them took a fag from my packet and lit up, jabbering away at the same time. I wasn't too pleased and scowled at them; they weren't speaking English so there was no point in saying anything. I felt a bit uneasy about it, but what are three fags?

My train came in late and disgorged its many passengers. The guard was trying to get his outgoing passengers on the train quickly so that he could be on his way, so I obliged him, left the café and boarded the train, ready for the off. Just before we moved I realised I'd left my paper and fags on the café table, so I jumped out and grabbed them just in the nick of time to jump back on the train as it was pulling out. The three men were still jabbering away and ran after me onto the platform, waving their arms as the train was leaving the station. I thought it was a bit odd that they didn't get on the train, but thought nothing of it until later when I decided to have a fag. On opening the packet I counted only six cigs – weird, there should be fifteen left after they'd nicked three. The ticket collector was checking tickets now so I went to get mine and there in my pocket was a packet of Rothmans cigs with just one missing. No wonder the men I left in the café were jabbering; I'd been smoking their cigs whilst all the time thinking that they were smoking mine and, to make matters worse, not only had I got my own cigs but I'd jumped back on the train with the rest of theirs as well. I felt terrible and if by any remote chance you read this lads (lads, they'll be old men just like me now) I owe you a big apology and a packet of fags. I can't remember the journey home, I must have fallen asleep.

Three months before, when I first came to work in Sheffield, I hated the smell of soot and the noise of the heavy machinery in Attercliffe, but now I was glad to get back to it and see friendly and smiling faces again. I missed London so much that it was twenty-four years before I went again. However, in all fairness, I have met and become great friends with lots of people from London since, but at that time I wasn't very worldly-wise and my little world finished just south of Sheffield.

I called at the Triangle fish shop in Handsworth, the best

in the area, and went back to my digs. It was too early to go to bed, so I nipped into the Norfolk Arms on Handsworth Road for a game of crib and snooker. It was a great pub and full of characters like Billy, Barry and Tommy, three tough lads. Even though I was a bobby and still wet behind the lug-holes, we got on like a house on fire. They were toughies alright, especially Tommy, and I wouldn't have fancied my chances against them, but luckily I never needed to.

When I got in the pub I could see that Len, as usual, was playing snooker. He was a man that I admired, always smartly dressed and with shoes polished, quietly spoken and always polite. I was hopeless at snooker then and still am today and the main reason that I admired Len was his tenacity and his brilliance at the table. I don't remember anyone beating him, which to me was amazing considering that he only had one arm.

The empty left sleeve of his jacket had a weight on the end and that and his sleeve fitted into his left-hand jacket pocket. With his right hand he placed the snooker rest into the crook of his left sleeve and took his shots using the rest which he placed on the cushion of the table, and for closer shots he used a small metal block with a groove in it which he put on the cushion. Good old Len, what a gentleman and what a player.

Three people came into the pub that I'd seen before, but I didn't know them to talk to. The woman was middle-aged and quite attractive and the two men were of a similar age. Whenever I saw them, which was usually on the Manor where I think they lived, they were always full of life and seemed happy. They intrigued me, so I asked one of the lads in the pub why they were always together. He pointed to one of the men and said, 'He's Monday, Wednesday and Friday and he' (pointing to the other guy) 'is Tuesday, Thursday and Saturday. On Sunday they all have a rest, it's called energy-saving.'

He looked serious when he spoke and because I was young and naive it took a while for the penny to drop and then I couldn't stop laughing; what a world.

I told the lads the story about the man and the stork which had them in stitches and as one of them said, 'Just imagine having a few beers, seeing that and then waking up with a hangover and remembering the stork. I'd give up supping because I would think I was seeing things.'

After having slept the clock round, almost, I went to the main police station and handed in my receipts and the inspector's change at the office. On my way out of the back door I dropped in on the inspector who'd sent me to London and told him that I'd left the receipts and change in the office.

'Thank you, Johnson.' Then, almost as an afterthought he said, 'Have you checked the duty rota for this week?' and he smiled as he then said, 'It's the early bird that catches the worm.' He stressed the word 'bird'.

When I looked at the rota I found that I was working the next seven afternoon shifts at Firth Park, the farthest point from where I lived and two bus rides each way, which would take about an hour to get to work and an hour to get back. I couldn't reckon it up and looked at the rota again to see who I was working with. It turned out to be PC 569 Terry Bruce, who lived further away than me at Woodhouse and probably three bus rides for him.

The 52 bus from Woodhouse pulled up the following day and as I got on I saw Terry near the front so went and sat with him. We swapped notes and Terry told me that one of the lads on the beat had called in at his house and told him that he had to work Firth Park and something about an 'early bird'.

When I told him that this is what the inspector said to me he started cursing. He had a lot more service in than me and he slowly shook his head.

'Punishment beat, pal – as far away as possible,' said Terry.

'What do you mean?' I asked.

'That's what they do if you've done owt wrong. If one of the lads at Firth Park had done owt wrong they'd have sent him to Woodhouse, his farthest point from home. That's our punishment.'

'For what?' I asked.

'The early bird,' answered Terry, shaking his head.

'I don't know what you mean,' I replied.

'I reckon the guy in the car who tried to shoo away our stork was the boss going into work early to get that parcel ready that you had to take to London. Punishment, pal, punishment. He could have sent one of the day-shift lads to London that morning, but decided to teach you a lesson.'

Thinking about it, I reckoned that he was right, the early bird was the boss going to work and we were the worms caught out and punished.

Ah well, another lesson learned the hard way, but at least we hadn't got the sack for our daft bit of fun.

CHAPTER SIX

The One That Got Away

By this time, as well as everyone working a foot patrol beat or a push-bike beat, the force had invested in two Ariel Leader 250cc motorcycles, used mainly to cover the larger outlying areas of the Division such as Woodhouse, The Manor, Firth Park and Parsons Cross, big areas containing tens of thousands of people.

Quite a few of us owned a motorbike as nobody in those days could afford a car and, because of this, I sometimes worked a motorbike beat. The volume of work we had to deal with was tremendous and we never had a minute. Unlike a foot beat, snap time sometimes only lasted five to ten minutes if you were lucky, especially on afters and our finishing time of 11pm was rarely achieved. All that to contend with and paid overtime did not exist; it was just part of the job. By then I'd completed my two years' probation, so qualified for a pay rise to the sum of £11 18s per week.

For that magnificent amount of money we had to deal with sudden deaths, suicides, traffic accidents, ambulance calls, pub fights, fires and all manner of things.

One of the jobs I hated the most was when dogs got hit by cars and were so badly injured that they had to be put down or destroyed. Vets weren't on call for this sort of situation then and nobody could afford to pay anyway, so it was down to us. We had to wait for someone to bring out the humane killer from the main police station, which could often mean a twenty-minute wait. Sometimes the owners of the dog and their children were there, but more often than not they weren't and there was a reason for this. Dogs had to be licensed then but 90 per cent weren't and the owners didn't want reporting, so they left the scene and the injured dog to await its fate alone.

Along with the humane killer, or catch bolt pistol, came a metal tube containing thick cord which formed a noose at one end. This allowed you to place the noose round the dog's head and restrain it somewhat in an attempt to stop it moving – a nightmare job on its own. The uncertainty of the next bit is what I hated.

The dogs were beyond all help and needed despatching quickly, so I had no qualms about it. You had to draw an imaginary line from the right ear to the left eye and then one from the left ear to the right eye. Where both lines crossed was supposedly the centre of the brain behind the poor dog's skull. The gun was placed on the cross and, when fired, shot the steel bolt through the skull and into the animal's brain.

Theory is one thing, fact another. If you got it right first time both you and the poor dog were lucky. If the bolt bounced off the skull or went in at an angle, the whole process had to be repeated to make sure that the dog was dead. I'd rather have strangled a dog with my own bare hands than use that humane thing, it was horrible. But there was no other way in those days. How anyone could call that humane is totally beyond me, and I hated it. Sorry if I've upset you but I'm telling you as it was; another part of a bobby's job that I could have done without.

By this time I felt more settled on the job. I've said it before and I'll say it again, I worked alongside some of the finest men and first-class bobbies that you could ever wish for. Between them they eased me into the job, for which I will always be grateful. They were proper men with big hearts. There were no textbooks written to prepare you for The Cliffe. We did what we felt was right and 99.9 per cent of the population were behind us. People felt safe.

A wise older chap, Sergeant Number 7, Les Seaton, once said to me 'I know you're not keen on knocking motorists off for petty offences, are you?'

I replied: 'No, Sergeant, I'm not. Serious offences yes, but not petty ones.'

'To keep the bosses off your back remember this: one good prisoner is worth a hundred petty motoring offences.' He then went on to say: 'The lads who knock off lots of motorists usually want to be in the Road Traffic Department and the lads with prisoners, the CID.' I didn't want to be in either, I loved working the beat, but I did bear it in mind. There was less paperwork (which I hated) when you caught prisoners for crimes, as the CID lads did most of that. The other benefit was that if you caught them 'bang to rights' (in the act), they usually pleaded guilty and you didn't have to faff about going to court.

A couple of years later I was to prove him right. When I started on the job I was shown round for three shifts and then you were on your own, but by this time it had changed and you were shown round for two weeks before going solo.

Another bobby and I had been shadowing a new and young recruit and showing him the ropes. He was always smiling and very amiable, as well as bright. All in all, a good lad and a quick learner.

Early one afternoon I was riding the police motorbike in Eleanor Street when, up in front of me, I saw PC Newbobby talking to the driver of a lorry which he had obviously just pulled up and stopped. Not wanting to interfere and embarrass him I pulled up alongside him and the driver, who I knew, and quietly asked if he needed any help.

'No thanks, I've got help on the way,' he replied. As I rode away I was dead chuffed for the lad; he'd just pulled up one of the middle-order scrap lads and, because of the nature of the lorry-load, I knew that it had to be knocked off. Good for you, mate.

Another hour on duty and then it would be home time. At about 2.50pm I was heading back to the nick when I suddenly noticed the same lorry go past me in the opposite direction and, as we passed, the driver and I looked at each other and then he smiled and waved. How odd. Why is he driving the lorry and not locked up? Only one way to find out and I turned to follow. He was nowhere to be seen. Five minutes to the end of shift and I was going to see my sister in Barnsley for her birthday, so which way should I jump? If I'm right I'll be late for my sister's birthday by some time. If I'm wrong then I'll not be too late. I had to know and rode up and down the road. Nothing. I'd lost him. Just then I realised that one of the big scrapyards was fairly near and I went to check it out.

Pulling in, I could see the lorry on the weighbridge. They wouldn't need a magnet for that load, it was non-ferrous in the form of round brass bars. When I saw him his face said it all and I could hear the silent 'f' words dying to get out.

'Your mate's already stopped me, so it's okay. He sent for some help and he's done me, so I'm in the clear. He's given me a producer, okay?' (A producer is a paper order to produce your tax, insurance and test certificate within seven days.)

68

'I'm not bothered about that. Where's the load from? Is it stolen?' I asked.

'You know it f —— is, you've had me before,' he replied angrily as he realised the game was up.

'Why did my mate let you go?'

'He sent for Road Traffic to check the wagon. They've done me for a bald tyre, faulty handbrake and a broken wing mirror. They never asked me about the load, so I thought I'd got away with it until you shoved yer f —— g sneck in.' I spoke to the owner of the yard who was watching us.

'Were you going to weigh him in?' I asked.

'No chance, the lad on the crane saw you from up there,' he said as he was pointing to the overhead crane. 'He said it looked like you were after somebody. Do I look like a dishonest man, officer?' He held his hands out palm upwards in front of him, shrugged his shoulders and gave me a wry smile. Won one, lost one. If he'd have let him weigh the metal in I could have had him for handling stolen property.

I arrested Mr Smile and Wave man and the CID lads dealt with the job. The value of the load was about thirty-five grand in today's money, a good arrest. For the life of me I can't remember what sentence he got so next time I see him, I'll ask him. I'm sure he'll remember that day better than me.

PC Newbobby was distraught when I told him what was what the day after, but with his short service I and some of the other lads may have done the same – or maybe not. He went on to spend most of his service in Road Traffic.

I was on my way home for my sister's birthday when I found a baby barn owl in the road with a broken wing, a beautiful bird and one of my favourites. I'd splinted a few hens' wings up on my dad's small allotment when I was younger and so I did the same with the owl and kept it in dad's shed for a few weeks before I took it back to where I'd found it for release, and off it went as good as new.

I was in bother with my sister and to make amends I later brought her to Sheffield for a Chinese meal as at that time there was no such thing where we lived and so it was a novelty for her.

A few weeks after locking up Mr Brass-Necked Thief, I was working the motorbike beat on nights in the Firth Park area of the Division. There'd been a spate of motorbike thefts from the city centre and all of them had been found dumped in Ecclesfield, just outside our Division, in the old West Riding Force. All had been stolen during the night and must be going through our Division to get to Ecclesfield and so we staked out the main road in Wincobank and waited. I was at the Wincobank end and the divisional car was nearer the city, on Carlisle Street.

An hour passed. Nothing apart from the odd car or two. Dawn was breaking and a few birds were starting to sing. We were in the industrial area of the city where all the steel-works were belching out smoke and the birds sounded as if they were smoking forty Park Drive fags a day, poor things.

Here we go, the radio of the bike crackled into life: 'Hello 49' (the bike call sign). 'Hello 49, we're following a motor-bike in your direction. The rider saw us and speeded up.'

It didn't have to be a bike with a big engine to outrun the divisional car, the Hillman Shooting Brake, but even so I knew that I had to somehow stop him because, in two min-utes or less, he'd be here and I had to be ready for him. I heard the roar of a car and a black Ford Zephyr Zodiac pulled up behind me. It was the Road Traffic lads who must have heard the message to me on their radio and, being nearby, had come to assist. One police car, one police motorbike and three policemen – he was ours.

PC Charlie Lampard, the driver of the police car, broad-sided his car across the road just in time and as the rider came over the brow of the hill he switched his blue light on and jumped back into his car ready for a chase, whilst I stood in the middle of the road and signalled him to stop.

The rider had long hair (no crash helmets required then) and at first I thought it might be a girl, but surely not on a motorbike. Panic was written on the rider's face and as the bike desperately tried to slow down I could see that it was a youth in jeans and an open-necked shirt. As he got nearer to us it was obvious that he couldn't stop in time and so he slid the bike from under him and, with sparks flying, he and the bike slid across some wasteland between The Railway and Engineers' pubs.

He was up like a shot and obviously not hurt as he legged it away from me. In those days I was as fit and strong as a butcher's dog and I was slowly gaining on him. Whenever I've chased anyone I've always watched the culprit as opposed to where they may be leading me, so that when he ran up some metal stairs I did the same and thought nothing of it. Believe me, this bloke could shift; he'd have beaten Roger Bannister in the first four-minute mile and I wouldn't have been far behind.

I stuck to him like glue and was slowly getting close enough to grab him. My heart, chest and head were pounding but I had to keep going, more steps, then on the level and then more steps. Where the hell were we? Would we ever stop? Then he just disappeared. After a couple of seconds I saw him sprinting across an almost level space and I froze.

Silhouetted against the dawn sky I could see the large buildings of the city stretching away in front of me in the distance. No trees or houses could be seen and, with a quaking and breathless voice, I whispered 'F ——— g hell'. Wearing two pairs of socks can make me feel dizzy and here I was on top of a gasometer of all places.

My next prisoner-to-be was now gone and I couldn't care

less. The view around me was great but when I looked down and saw Charlie, the Zephyr Zodiac and the Hillman Husky I went as dizzy as a spinning top and swore again. Heights don't bother some people but they hate going underground. The opposite applied to me, I'd been down a pit several times and had even been potholing but heights were something else. Eventually I got down but really had to steel myself to do so and when I got to the bottom I had a fag in each hand and shook like a rabid dog.

The bike had been stolen and the thief was gone, but a few weeks later he was caught by another shift and admitted to stealing all the other bikes.

We've all driven past loads of gasometers in our lives including you, but being a thicko meant that until that day I hadn't realised that they grew in height the more gas was in them.

Please, if just one reader admits to themselves that they didn't know either it would make me feel a lot better – just let me know.

I still felt dizzy when I got home. A pot of tea calmed me down a bit but when I went to bed I fell out three times just dreaming about it. Ah well.

CHAPTER SEVEN

Sergeant Turd and a Mystery Man

It was Friday morning and nice and sunny as I worked the foot beat between Darnall and Handsworth. After today it was my weekend off and then on Monday I was going up to Strensall Army Barracks, near York, for a week with a Police Mobile Column, to travel round the north of England with them. I was looking forward to both.

Just as I got into the police box, the phone rang. On answering it the duty sergeant at Attercliffe said that an ambulance had been called to an address on Handsworth Road and would I attend. The address concerned was fairly near and as I looked out of the dark-blue glass windows I could see the ambulance pull up outside the house. Attending the house I could see an old gentleman being brought out on a stretcher and the ambulance man told me that he was in a bad way, and off they drove. A neighbour outside the house gave me his details and also told me that he was too mean to buy food and that he'd collapsed from malnourishment.

It looked clean enough inside the house but the only food the neighbour and I saw was a crust of dry bread and an empty milk bottle.

'Has he any relatives nearby?' I asked, then said, 'I'll have to inform them.'

'I think he has a nephew who works on the buses, but I haven't a clue where he lives.' The neighbour locked the door and I went back to inform the office of the circumstances of the call. I knew what they would say.

'Is the house secure?' the sergeant asked.

'Yes, Sergeant,' I replied.

'Relatives informed?'

'No, Sergeant, whereabouts unknown at this stage.'

'If the man dies on the way to the hospital, then you'll have to fetch the body and take it to the mortuary. If I don't ring you at your next point he will have survived and will be the responsibility of the hospital. Okay?'

My next point was the phone box near the top of Finchwell Road and I stood outside hoping that the phone wouldn't ring. I obviously didn't want the old man to die and luckily the phone kept quiet.

At this time I was courting my lovely wife-to-be Christine

and we were going to my mum and dad's for the weekend before I went to Strensall the following week.

We had a stroll round the village of Darfield, and I showed her the old house we used to rent on Vicar Lane and the allotment where my sister Bronnie and I used to feed our three pigs and a few hens. I lived in Vicar Lane until I was five. It was just after the war, when most things were on ration. My memories of childhood were all happy ones. On Sunday afternoons after tea we would all go into the front room, which was not used during the week, and mum, dad and grandma would make peggy rugs. There was a large wooden frame with hessian cloth stretched tightly across it and, while my sister and I cut up clippings from old clothes, mum and dad would use a pointed tool to weave the clippings into lovely patterns which, when finished, were used to cover up the stone kitchen floor and bedrooms. Being the eldest child, it was my job to wind up an old gramophone which stood in the corner of the room and, if you wound the handle when a record was already on the turntable it made the singers' voices go faster, which had us all in stitches.

Everybody helped each other in those days, and as I got older and bigger I would get home from school and either mum or dad would say, 'Just nip to Mrs So-and-So's house and put her coal in the coal shed, please. Tea will be ready in an hour.'

All coal miners had a yearly coal ration which was delivered and tipped in a pile on the pavement outside the recipient's house. If the husband had died his widow would receive nine one-ton loads of coal per year. When the coal was dumped it had to be put in the coal shed quickly before anyone fell over it in the dark. The old ladies were of course very grateful and offered to pay.

'It's all right, Mrs So-and-So, I'll have to go because my tea will be ready,' I would say and that's how it was and that's how it should be. What goes round comes round, and we were brought up to help people.

Christine's mum and dad, Mabel and Albert Mills, caught the bus from Sheffield on the Sunday and after tea my dad took them to the British Legion Club where they all enjoyed a game of bingo and a good laugh. No one had a car then and we caught the last bus back to Sheffield and home.

Strensall Army Barracks was a huge complex of buildings, including a parade ground and dormitories in the form of large Nissan huts, and a large assault course used for training purposes, the first I'd ever seen.

There were policemen from all the major cities in the North taking part in the training exercise and we all possessed different skills. Our role was to be a Mobile Police Unit, or Column, ready to be sent in a fleet of old Thames Trader lorries to anywhere in the North that had suffered a nuclear or terrorist attack. Having been a blacksmith before joining the force, I became a rescue leader and had to improvise the use of whatever was available to make stretchers for anyone injured and also anything else that may be needed.

The attitude of the Army lads towards us being on their base was apparent. They didn't like the police and resented our presence. They were very fit with all the training they did and they thought that we were like big girls' blouses and soft.

It transpired that we'd taken over three of their billet huts or dormitories and each contained forty men, which meant that they had to move 120 men somewhere else on camp. They didn't like it.

The following morning we all woke early and the first lad out of the billet trod right into a pile of shit right outside the door. It hadn't been there the night before and the fenced-off compound had no animals in it, so it had to be human excrement. We were off camp each day doing what we were there to do and on our arrival back at camp one or two soldiers, along with a sergeant, were making snide comments aimed at us. Several of us wanted to have a go back but being guests on the Army base forced us to resist the temptation.

The following two mornings were the same, with a 'present' left for us on the doorstep – we'd got the message.

Outside the door to all the billets was a narrow concrete path with a fairly small privet hedge at either side and now I was hiding behind one of them and waiting. Brain was better than brawn and, even though I'd been born with more of the latter, I'd got a plan and I couldn't wait. I've always loved a bit of mischief and a laugh and if I got the timing right, bingo. By prior arrangement with our lads, the lights in our billet were out and the only light on was the one over the door and it was shining on the path.

Fifteen minutes, twenty minutes and then, creeping on tiptoe appeared the phantom – Mr Turd. As he got nearer and under the light I could see that it was the sergeant himself and he looked grumpy, with a face that even a dog wouldn't lick. I'd borrowed a shovel from one of the lorries and wrapped cloth around the metal blade so as not to make a noise – get ready mate.

He obviously thought we were all asleep and, with a toilet roll in one hand, he managed to drop his trousers and underpants and then got into a crouching position. You know the one. That was my cue and I grasped the shovel in both hands. If I had made a noise I'd have blown it, so very carefully I slid the shovel through the privet hedge until the blade rested just under his bum – perfect. I didn't have long to wait and there in a neat pile on my shovel was my evidence. As soon as the paper arrived I deftly pulled the shovel back through the hedge and waited with a hanky in my mouth to stop me laughing out loud.

As I slid further back into the shadows, I knew that our lads in the billet would be watching. The now chuckling sergeant pulled up his trousers and, as is human nature, turned round to look at the proceeds of his actions. Nothing. He wasn't chuckling now. The look on his face was amazing, first he looked left and then to his right and still nothing; he looked dazed and stunned as he scratched his head. His mind must have been working overtime; all that effort and nothing to see for it, he knew he'd done something but where was it? I was rolling about on the floor behind the hedge, inwardly screaming with laughter. Stage two to follow.

The sergeant walked away but then came back for another look round. He couldn't reckon it up and then he went, still scratching his head and muttering. Back in our billet the lads were hysterical and I got more than a few pats (pardon the pun) on the back. Some of the lads then took the shovel containing the evidence across to the billet where Sergeant Turd slept and deposited the contents on *his* doorstep.

Early the next morning saw a few of us back at the sergeant's billet to see what the reaction might be, but we watched from a distance until the door was opened and the soldiers came out.

They came out of the door and were watching us approach instead of looking where they were going when one of them walked straight into it and started cursing because it was all over his parade boots. How I wished that it had been their sergeant who trod in it instead of them.

As we casually walked passed the sergeant, our inspector

said, 'Good morning, Sergeant.' His face looked like an angry wasp and his eyes were bulging. The eyes narrowed as he stared at our boss, not sure of what to say because of his higher rank. Nodding towards the pile of excrement the inspector said, 'Must have been a big man and desperate for the loo to do that on your doorstep, Sergeant.' He knew the game was up and visibly relaxed as he said to the boss, 'Okay, you lads have played us at our own game and got your own back, but what the hell happened last night?' The Inspector beckoned me across and said, 'Ask this young man here, I'm sure he'll tell you.'

As the circumstances of his midnight ablutions started to unfold, everyone, including our lads and the soldiers, started laughing and, to give him his due, none more so than the sergeant.

'Thank bloody goodness for that, I couldn't sleep last night. When I did what I did and turned round and saw that there was nothing there, I thought I was losing my marbles.' And with that he grabbed my hand and shook it. 'Brilliant; brilliant.' He kept saying 'brilliant', he must have said it twenty times. He laughed and shook his head at what he'd heard. During the rest of the week things were very different. Instead of being enemies we were now all pals together and the following year when we had to go back, we were welcomed with open arms.

*

By coincidence, when I got back to normal duties the very first job I was given was to go back to the house in Handsworth where the old man had to be hospitalised because of malnutrition. Unfortunately he had passed away half an hour before, and the hospital contacted us in the hope that we could somehow trace a relative to release the body to, in order for them to make burial arrangements.

Knocking on the neighbour's door, I took off my helmet as I told her of the man's death. She was very upset. Apparently he used to say that he couldn't afford food.

'I've known him for eight years, Officer and, as far as I know, he's no friends or visitors apart from me. He visits the post office once a week for his pension and then, I assume, he buys some food. He sits in the dark and listens to his wireless and he even has a shilling [5p] in the slot meter for his gas and electric.'

'He must have a relative somewhere,' I said.

'I know him better than anyone, but still know nothing about him at all really, love. As I told you, when he was first taken to hospital, he once mentioned a nephew on the buses but I've never seen him or anyone else visit him in eight years. He was a reclusive old man.'

I explained to her the reason for my visit, at the same time asking if she still had the key to next door which she offered to me. She was reluctant to go into the house with me but I explained that I needed to go through his belongings in order to, hopefully, find a name and address of a possible relative and that I needed someone with me as a witness. We both entered the house together and both of us admitted to feeling uneasy about doing so. It seemed almost irreverent with the owner being dead. Where do you start? Clothing, drawers, cupboards? It was anyone's guess.

Agnes, the neighbour, went to look in a drawer and within seconds she let out a gasp.

'Come and look at this, Officer.' She'd opened a large old exercise book and inside were ten white £5 notes which we placed on the table. At this point I picked up another old book and out popped a dozen crumpled white fivers, which, along with another twenty-two that Agnes found loose in the same drawer, made up one hell of a lot of money for those days. It was the same in the next drawer, and within five minutes of starting the search we had found well over £1,000 plus a cloth bag full of gold sovereigns, but still nothing with a name or address on it.

At that time £1,000 represented two years' pay for me, and neither Agnes nor I could believe what was happening, especially when I noticed the old crust of bread and empty milk bottle from just over a week ago, the only food in the house.

Realising that we may have to search the house more thoroughly before we found details of a relative (if any) and due to the possibility of finding more money, I decided to lock up and seek assistance.

The post office was fairly near and I knew that they would have a telephone. When I got there I phoned the main police station, outlined the circumstances to the inspector and he told me that he would send a sergeant to meet me at the house. I was to ask the postmaster to accompany me in order to collate and record any further monies found. His presence there would also give us corroboration if required.

Sergeant Horsfield, the postmaster, Agnes and I entered the house again and renewed the search. Wherever we looked there was money, and war bonds from about twenty years ago. None of us, even collectively, had ever seen as much money and 90 per cent of it was in used white £5 notes. In magazines, vases, cups, behind cushions, you name it, there were loads of them, but nothing at all to give us a lead to any relative, not even a bank book.

At this point the sergeant got the CID lads out and when they saw the pile of fivers on the table their eyes stuck out like chapel hat pegs. At that point my services were no longer required, so me and Agnes went to her house for a well-earned pot of tea and a fag. We hardly spoke and just sat with our own thoughts, shaking our heads in disbelief at what we'd seen.

A few days later I was told that the detectives had found several newspaper cuttings relating to a robbery in London during the Second World War. They made enquiries at Scotland Yard and discovered that this particular robbery involved the theft of used white £5 notes to the value of about £70,000. This was a huge sum of money in those days and at today's value worth well over £2,000,000. Furthermore, no money had ever been recovered and not only was no one arrested for doing the robbery but no one was even shown as a suspect; they had no idea who had done the job and committed the robbery and the case had been closed.

We never found a relative and I assume that the cash that we recovered eventually went to the government. If our mystery man had indeed been the armed robber he'd covered his tracks well, but not being sure of that at the time he probably daren't spend any of his ill-gotten gains in case it drew attention to him. What a waste.

CHAPTER EIGHT

Little Boy in 'Blue'

Working the night shift on a foot beat was just my cuppa tea and especially during the week. A bit of argy-bargy during the first hour when people were leaving the pubs and a couple of domestics (family squabbles); and then everyone was snoring away ready for work in the morning.

The shops around Darnall Terminus were all secure, but the tobacconist's had been broken into a couple of weeks before and a large amount of fags nicked. There was a brick wall about six feet high surrounding the backyard of the building and we couldn't see over the top of it to check the rear of the premises. That meant that anyone could break in at the back without being seen. Borrowing an empty wooden crate from the greengrocers, I shinned over the wall and shone my torch round the yard. I'd never been able to access the yard before and at the rear of the premises I saw a metal cage fastened to the back wall of the shop. It had a switch at the side which I pressed without thinking. First came a whirring noise and then what looked like a large box within the cage moved slowly up the wall on wire ropes, which I hadn't noticed before.

At 1am it made me jump but when it reached the second floor I jumped again as the burglar alarm activated and I twigged that the cage was a small loading lift – too late. Because it was high-value stock the alarm had sent a signal to the main nick and the poor owner had to leave his warm bed and reset the alarm. When he arrived I explained what had happened and why and he was over the moon knowing that we were doing our job as it should be done and, after thanking me, gave me twenty Rothman cigarettes; fancy getting a tip for making a mistake.

The next job was to check the banks on the Terminus. Two of the older banks had frosted glass in the door. There was a two-inch diameter circle of clear glass in the middle of the frosted glass to enable us to look through, and directly in our eye line was the safe. The safe had a light above it so that it was clearly visible from the door. We could check that it was still intact and had not been tampered with in any way and all was well.

I nipped into the public urinal on the Terminus and saw the graffiti on the wall with the aid of my torch. The piece of graffiti that caught my eye made me laugh. Someone had written: 'I love grils'. Someone else had written underneath: 'Surely you mean girls'. Then underneath that some smart alec had written: 'But what about us poor grils'. It made me chuckle all night long.

The kettle was on the boil when I called into Ike Worral's bakehouse on Main Road and as I was mashing I swapped my uniform jacket for a white smock in order to help Ike for half an hour before my 2.15am early snap time in the police box. There was a flour shortage at the time and bread was being rationed, so I asked Ike to put six small white loaves in bags for me. I know what you're thinking and that's where you're wrong. They weren't for me, and I later left one each on the back door knobs of different elderly people's houses on my patch. They were old or infirm, and must have believed in a 'floury godmother' because I never did let on it was me who had left the bread.

Cold fish sandwiches with a touch of vinegar might not be everybody's cup of tea but I loved them, especially followed by two bananas, a pint pot of tea and a fag. At 3am I was back on the beat and checking the shops for break-ins.

There were fewer vehicles about in those days and any good old bobby knew what was on his patch. It was a fair walk down Poole Road to the dog track and I couldn't work out what anyone would steal if they broke in there, but even so it had to be dutifully checked and I found it secure. Next was the wholesale chemist's in Creswell Road. It was set back from the road and away from the gas lamp and at that time I wasn't to know that a lovely little lass (a friend of ours called Mandy) would later work there. Again all was well, but further down the road I noticed a large blue van which I'd not seen parked there before and so I went to investigate.

It was as black as midnight apart from the one dim gaslight, but I didn't switch on my torch in case someone saw the light. After creeping down the side of the van and looking through the front side windows, I could see that there was no one inside. Feeling the bonnet with my hand told me that the engine was hot so it must be a recent arrival. I climbed onto the rear bumper, cupped the torch in my hand and peered through the back window. You'd have thought it was a mobile off-licence. There were boxes of whisky, gin, rum and brandy all in there waiting to be supped. Could it be knocked off? A few houses down from the chemist's I could see a light coming from the fanlight above the front door. As I crept nearer I could hear muffled voices coming from within the house but couldn't see anyone because of the thick curtains. I sneaked down the passage between the houses but all was dark at the back of the house. What next? Come on, lad – think, think, think.

After using my noggin to think with, I quietly ran back to the dog track where there were some old garages nearby. After rummaging about I found what I was looking for – a fairly large piece of broken mirror glass. I made my way back to the house where I quietly stood with my back to the front door. Slowly, I raised the mirror until I could see through the glass fanlight above the door and into the front room.

There were two middle-aged men sitting at a table, each with a small glass containing what looked like whisky. I saw them raise and clink the glasses together as though they were toasting some sort of success. As I looked beyond them I saw several large boxes with writing on them in large letters: Senior Service, Park Drive, Kensitas, Woodbine; and also Rothman and that's when it hit me.

If I left the house now and turned right onto the footpath under the railway bridge and then down the alley, I would come out at the side of the tobacconist's shop where I had set off the alarm only four hours ago, literally just a three-minute walk from where I was standing. If my hunch was correct I was in for a decent arrest but, being on my own, that was easier said than done.

My mind and heart were racing. The phone box was about a third of a mile away, but I had to risk it. If the men came out and drove off while I was away I'd lose them. The odds of two to one in a scrap didn't bother me, having seen them both, but I could still lose them and, therefore, I had to be quick. My feet didn't touch the floor as I ran down to the telephone kiosk. (If only someone had invented a phone that you could carry about!) We were all issued with four brass tokens the same size and weight as an old penny so, using them, I rang the nick and asked for assistance, but no blue-light stuff.

The cavalry, in the form of a uniformed sergeant and the night detective, arrived and we hid in the shadows and waited and waited and waited. You couldn't check the registration number against the owner of the vehicle like you can today, so we had to wait until they got into the van before we made a move. Both the sergeant and Sherlock Holmes complimented me for my observation and agreed that what we had seen must be bent (stolen) gear.

After nearly two hours the men left the house and got into the van but before they moved away the sergeant and I pulled open the doors, switched off the engine and removed the ignition key. To say that they were shocked would be an understatement and in fact one of them put his hands up in the air just like in the old movies. They didn't look or act like normal burglars; they made no attempt to escape and just sat there trembling. I'm sure if I'd shouted 'boo' both would have fainted.

Sherlock Holmes, the detective, asked them where the stuff in the van was from and the heavier of the two said, very politely, 'I've stolen it all from where I used to work.' He mentioned a large warehouse on the edge of Sheffield.

'When did you steal it?' the detective asked.

'Tonight. I used to be the manager and I've got a bad heart

and had to have time off, so they sacked me three weeks ago,' he replied.

'Is that why you broke in?'

'I didn't break in. Before I left I copied all the keys including the alarm key and the gate key. I've been stupid, I know. Until then I hadn't stolen anything in my life.'

Sherlock cautioned him and told him he was under arrest and his reply was, 'I've also bought a load of fags off two chaps which I know were stolen.'

The smaller bloke was trembling like a jelly when the detective spoke to him.

'What have you got to do with all this?'

'We were just taking it all to my shop to sell.'

He was cautioned and arrested and his reply was, 'I'm the same as him, never done owt wrong in my life but I could have made a good few quid on that lot, so I went for it, sorry.'

All the gear was later deposited along with Laurel and Hardy at Attercliffe police station.

The little guy had paid Mr Ex-manager for the goods and he was charged with handling stolen property, a more serious offence than the theft of it. No handlers, no thieves.

Although I had a lot less service in than the sergeant or detective, even I knew that none of us would ever again deal with an easier arrest, admission and recovery of all property; it was laughably simple. The detective later went on to arrest the two chaps who had broken into the tobacconist's and stolen the fags in the first place. They weren't happy that they'd been grassed up by an amateur handler, or fence, but that was their hard luck.

Laurel was charged with the theft of the booze and handling stolen property (cigs) and Hardy with handling the stolen cigs and booze. As daft as anything, they were both decent chaps with no previous convictions. Both pleaded guilty and were very, very genuinely remorseful, resulting in a suspended prison sentence or a slap on the wrist, which meant that if they kept their noses clean (out of trouble) for two years they would have, in effect, got away with it.

The headline in the *Star* read: 'Sharp-eyed PC Spots Booze Loot in Van' and I received a commendation from the Chief Constable to boot. It was a late finish for me the morning of that arrest and I was ravenous, but when I got back to my digs I couldn't believe it; I'd forgotten to get a loaf for my landlady Mrs Proctor, so ended up with a boiled egg but no bread soldiers with it.

If I had been working the area on a motorbike or in a Panda car the arrest and recovery of the stolen property would have been highly unlikely and our two amateur burglars would have gone on to commit more crimes, thinking it was easy.

All bobbies in my day would tell you that every shift brought something different and you never knew until that something happened that it was unusual in some way.

A few weeks after the arrest of Laurel and Hardy, I was working the same beat down The Cliffe as the one where I'd caught the coal thief with the squeaky pram (see Chapter 1 of *What's Tha Up To?*) a few years before. At about 4am I was checking property on Newhall Road when I heard 'squeak, squeak, squeak' again just like before. Not again, I thought, and then suddenly out of the darkness and into the light of a streetlamp I saw him. He was pedalling away on the pavement and coming straight towards me, very slowly. Standing in his path, I knelt down and took off my helmet as I didn't want to alarm him and he stopped in front of me. I could tell from his face that I was more surprised at seeing him than he was at seeing me.

He looked to be about five years old and was in a toy car with metal pedals that you push backwards and forwards to make it move. I couldn't believe my eyes. What was he doing out and alone at this time of the morning and how had he got here?

'Hello young fella, are you going for a little drive?' I gently asked.

'I'm going to my grandma's,' he replied.

'Where does your grandma live, do you know?'

'I think so.'

'What's your name?'

'Max.'

He was totally relaxed and happy, and even tried to

94

manoeuvre his little car around me in order to continue his journey to his grandma's.

'How old are you Max, do you know?'

'Five, but daddy says I'll be six soon.'

'Do you know where you live?'

'In a right big house,' he answered, and he lifted both his little arms up in the air to demonstrate how big the house was and then continued, 'Are you a real policeman?'

'I think so, Max, yes.'

'What's your name?'

'PC Johnson.'

'Do you live at the police station?'

'Yes, I do.' It was easier to say yes and at this point I was laughing and wondering who was interviewing who. He was a proper lad alright. I tried to regain some dignity by asking the next question.

'Would you like to see a police car and a police station?' His eyes lit up.

'Yes please, but I'm a bit tired, will you carry me?'

'Come on then, off we go.'

He still had his pyjamas on but no shoes and as I picked him up with one arm and his little car with the other he put his head on my shoulder which gave me a wonderful warm feeling and it was at this point that I decided I would love to have some kids of my own.

By the time I'd walked the half a mile to the police station little Max was fast asleep on my shoulder. You could have heard a pin drop in the station when I got there. All the lads, except me, were fathers and if I heard the word 'shush' once, I heard it a hundred times from the lads, the sergeant, the inspector and Barbara Greaves, our lovely telephonist, as she took over. A prisoner in the old cells was shouting and bawling until the inspector went in and shut him up.

One by one the lads disappeared and came back with a comic or sweets from the paper shop and when little Max woke up there was a big pile of sweets on the table for him. There were no reports of a child missing anywhere and we rightly assumed that mum and dad must still be asleep and blissfully unaware that little Max had gone missing. We were all due to finish at 7am but the inspector, Barbara and I stayed on to await the outcome.

The expected phone call came in at about 7.30am. His hysterical mother had run to a phone box and rung 999 and reported little Max missing. He could have lived anywhere in the city, so we had alerted all divisions telling them to wait for the call. The call came to West Bar police station and his mum was told that he was safe and in 'police custody' and that he would be home soon, now that we knew where he lived.

The inspector was like a little kid himself as he put the blue light on for Max before he put him in the police car to take him home, a good two miles by road; no wonder the little lad had fallen asleep on my shoulder after all that ped-alling. It turned out that he lived on the top floor of a block of flats (hence his description of a big house). We looked after him so well that he did the same thing again, we were told, a few weeks later and was found in a different part of the city. He must have enjoyed our company because he asked the lads for some sweets and a ride back home in the police car, but who could blame him?

Like all the emergency services, you never knew what your next call would bring, which is why we remember them so well. The nature of the job was so varied that no two jobs were ever the same.

CHAPTER NINE

A Lucky Escape?

Seven o'clock couldn't come soon enough for me and I was quite excited. I was working 3pm to 11pm down Attercliffe and the observer in the Hillman Husky Shooting Brake or divisional patrol car was to finish at 7pm so that he could start his annual leave a bit early. I had been told by the inspector to take over his duties.

In order to obtain those dubious duties you had to have served at least four years on the beat and, even though I hadn't, for the sake of four hours only I'd been given the opportunity as I'd never done it before. I was looking forward to it, especially so as I would be riding shotgun with my mate PC Tony Garnett.

Nothing much happened in the first three hours of my shift and I'd called in to see Jim at the herbalist's shop on

Attercliffe Road. The first time I went in was to see what they sold as I'd never seen one before and I found it fascinating. It was full of chemist's jars with weird names on them, as well as pills and potions of every description. The kids would call in for a penny stick of 'Spanish' (which looked like a twig off a tree to me) or a liquorice stick or a bag of tiger nuts. People would come in the shop for cures of all descriptions, including constipation, head-aches, piles, nausea, acne, ringworm, scabies and loads more ailments. I never knew whether Jim was a qualified chemist or a quack doctor, but he seemed to have a cure for every-thing.

Jim was a nice man who worked in his little shop for at least twelve hours every day, seven days a week. He also sold something I'd never heard of: Vimto and sarsaparilla, which I loved and it helped cut into the dirty clack you breathed in from the many steelworks. There was, to me, something mys-tical about Jim, his shop and his customers and I often spent twenty minutes or so with him.

The Hillman Husky had a blue light on top and a tele-phone handset inside, exactly the same as the old black ones in telephone kiosks. My job was to use the radio while Tony drove, and also to be observant. We covered a huge area, from Halifax Road at Parsons Cross and right across to Woodhouse Mill about ten miles away, and everything in between. It was vast and comprised of houses, works and shops containing tens of thousands of people, no wonder we were rushed off our feet with work.

At about 10.30pm and with just half an hour to go before the end of the shift, we got a call to attend a domestic disturbance in Grimesthorpe about five miles away from where we were.

'Here we go again,' said Tony. 'Put that light on.' At one point the old car got to nearly 60mph, which was fast then. We got to the house and could hear a man and woman shouting at each other and swearing.

Going down the dark entry, the open back door revealed a couple in their forties rowing like mad. The woman had a swollen eye where he'd obviously clipped her. He looked a nasty piece of work and he was snarling at her and raising his arm to hit her again. Violence is, and always will be, part of the job and you have to learn how to handle it and sometimes to use it yourself and, in a split second, I had his arm up his back and a stranglehold round his neck.

As I dragged him down the passageway to the car the woman was screaming, 'Please don't let him come back, he's always hitting me. Here's his case,' she pleaded and passed Tony a suitcase. Once at the car he calmed down and I released the hold. At this time the case was on the pavement and for some reason Tony said, 'Anyway, what's in your case?' The man didn't react and again Tony said, 'What's in your case? Open it.'

To us it was a 'ten-a-penny' domestic which we dealt with all the time, but when he went to open the case all that changed.

In the darkness, he slowly bent down, flicked the catches open on the case and stood up. We were looking down the barrel of a revolver which was only a few inches from our faces. Questions bounced around my head. Was it real? We didn't know. Was it loaded? We didn't know. Would he use it? We didn't know. How long did we stand there? We didn't know. What should we do? We didn't know. What could we do? We didn't know.

When you think you are going to die, all these thoughts go through your mind in a flash and I wondered if Jim at the herbalist had a cure for diarrhoea.

At some point, which could have been a second, a minute or an hour later, the man started to lower the gun but with it still pointing at us. Slowly, he moved it in my direction and it was pointing right at my stomach, when suddenly Tony let fly with his right fist, which caught Billy the Kid clean on the chin and he flew backwards over a low wall. I followed him and grabbed the gun which he'd dropped and then, between us, we managed to handcuff him, take him back to the station and put him in the cells.

The duty sergeant was Tom Coulthard, an old-timer who everyone respected. Three years before he got a call to attend the East House pub on Spital Hill where three men had been shot. He attended the pub on his own, saw the carnage and asked the landlord how many bullets had been fired. 'Four,' said the landlord.

'That means he's got two left then; where's the man gone?' Tom asked.

'He's shut himself in the outside toilet; he knows the police are coming.'

With that, Tom knocked on the toilet door telling the man to come out. Nothing happened and so Tom kicked the door in and dragged the man out, gun and all, including two live rounds. Not to be recommended, but that's what he did. He arrested a murderer with a loaded gun, single-handed.

'What have you arrested him for, lads?' Sergeant Coulthard asked. Tony told him the story and passed him the gun. The old sergeant looked at the gun and said, 'It's too heavy for a real gun, it must be a toy,' and he promptly threw the gun in the bin, much to our amazement.

'Is anybody hurt?' he asked.

'His chin and my hand,' replied Tony.

'Serves him right,' said Tom, 'bring him out here.' We got him from the cells and the sergeant gave him a right shouting at, finishing with the words, 'Guns will get you in bother, lad. We haven't time to deal with idiots like you, so my men are going to take you to the city boundary and drop you off. Never come near Sheffield again or you'll be arrested. Okay?'

The prisoner nodded his assent.

Neither Tony nor I could believe what we were hearing, but in those days you did as you were told. We did just that and dropped him off near Swallownest, along with his suitcase, minus gun of course.

Christine, my wife-to-be, and I used to babysit for Tony Garnett and his wife Theresa. Their kids were Jimmy, John and Julie, a lovely family. Every time we met and even now, forty-seven years later, we still get on about the sergeant's decision, but things worked differently then – for the better, I think.

Relating this story has reminded me of another odd one, so I might as well tell you about that too.

I'd got about two years' service in in 1964 and I was working foot patrol on Attercliffe Common, on nights. It had been a fairly quiet night and my snap time was 3.15am to 4am. Earlier that day I'd called to see Mr Tsang at the Chinese Laundry to pick up my starched uniform shirt collars. His English was pretty limited, a bit like my Barnsley English, but we seemed to get by.

'Ah, Johnson, you come.' And he beckoned me into the back of the shop where his wife was cooking. 'You sit, eat,' and he passed me two chopsticks. At this time I'd never had a Chinese meal and I held a chopstick in each hand like I would hold a knife and fork until they both laughed and showed me what to do, even though I ended up using a spoon. The food, whatever it was (I think fish) was delicious, and they insisted that I took some home. Over the years they taught me a smattering of Cantonese and even now I can order a takeaway in Chinese which amazes and amuses the shopkeepers.

The lads at the police station were all sniffing the air when I put the rest of my Chinese meal in a pan and heated it up. It beat potted-meat sandwiches any day.

'Johnson, it's nearly 4am, come on, we've got a job.' It was Inspector Sam Radford, another old-timer and he was in charge of the whole shift. He was waiting near the office and talking to a lady of about fifty who was in a nightdress covered with a long coat and she sounded very upset. I heard the inspector say, 'We'll walk down with you, don't worry.' As we set off I was behind him and I picked up from their conversation what was happening and where we were going.

The lady lived down Alfred Road where, a few years ago, the infamous Alfred Road gang hung out. It was almost a mile from the station and it had a cobbled road lit by gas lamps and wasn't a very salubrious place to live. I could hear the lady keep saying, 'It's a miracle, it's a miracle.' And it took the length of the walk before I knew what she was on about.

At about 4pm on the previous afternoon the lady was getting tea ready for her and her husband, who had just finished work on early days, when suddenly the back door opened to reveal their son, aged about twenty-five years old. He looked a bit agitated and upset but they welcomed him with open arms and were overcome and crying with emotion at the same time.

He was their only child and, at the age of seventeen, he left the house to go and buy some cigarettes and they'd never seen or heard from him since and, quite naturally, assumed that he must be dead. They were over the moon and ecstatic at his return, as any parent would be, seeing him again after eight years. He had an injury to one of his hands and seemed on edge but, after tea and a few beers, everyone went to bed, but they still didn't know anything about his whereabouts over the missing years.

In the early hours they were woken by banging and shouting and came downstairs to find their son smashing up the house and demanding cigarettes. They could also see that he was frothing at the mouth. His dad had found him some cigs which he smoked quickly, one straight after the other. When the fags had gone he kicked off again and when he started throwing things about the poor woman fled the house to phone us. The payphone at the end of Liverpool Street wasn't working, so she had to run all the way to the police station for help, poor lass.

The divisional car was tied up on another job which is why we also had to walk to the house. As we got nearer, a few neighbours could be seen near the house having been woken by the din, which we could also hear. Not knowing what to expect, the inspector told me to follow him into the house and to keep an eye on the lady, who was crying, just in case.

As we entered through the off-shot kitchen and into the main room I could see a couple of broken chairs and broken pottery lying about. A man, who was obviously the dad, was cowering in a corner looking terrified and the younger man was mooching round the kitchen, mumbling to himself. His eyes were wild and he was frothing at the mouth. When he saw us he said, 'Give me a cigarette – give me a cigarette.' A nod from the inspector said to do it and so I passed him a Rothman's. I enjoyed a fag myself and thought it might calm him down a bit but he just grabbed it and lit it and I couldn't believe the next bit as he took a big breath, sucked on the fag and kept sucking until he was blue in the face. The cig was almost gone with one big puff and then the rest of it, still lit, he popped in his mouth and chewed it!

As this was happening I could see his hand which held the fag – the flesh was various colours of black and green, and two of his fingers had no flesh on at all, just the bones, and it was obvious that his hand was gangrenous. At this point he snarlingly asked for another fag and, when I refused, he started to roar and then in an act of, I assume, defiance he pushed his gangrenous hand into his mouth.

Poor old mum and dad were distraught and in tears. A few hours before, their only son had appeared out of the blue after going missing for eight years and now they were witness to this horrible situation. None of us there that night needed to be a detective or brain surgeon to work out that the poor man was mentally deranged and needed treatment for that and for his hand.

He was screaming for cigarettes and bellowing as well as throwing things about, including his poor old dad. The inspector nodded to me and I knew what he meant – grab him. He must have realised what was coming and, as I went round the other side of the table, he picked up a large kitchen knife in one hand and a poker in the other. The inspector shouted mum and dad to leave the house so that they didn't get injured. You're right, it was scary alright, but he wasn't that big or powerful and, as he lunged at the inspector with the knife, I grabbed a cast-iron kettle off the table and knocked the knife out of his hand and then we both rushed him. A blow from the poker thankfully hit me on the helmet and at that point we overpowered and cuffed him. The inspector asked someone to go to the station, and to bring the Hillman patrol car to assist.

Back at the station, he was put into the cells where he kept asking for cigarettes and stuffing his gangrenous hand in his mouth. An ambulance and a DAO (Duly Authorised Officer under the Mental Health Act) were sent for, but on arrival the ambulance crew wouldn't carry him; he was too dangerous and there was no DAO on duty.

The inspector was going crackers about the lack of support and contacted Middlewood Hospital, which dealt with such cases. Luckily for us they agreed to look at him if we could get him there. The divisional driver and I took him to the medical unit where the poor lad was placed in a straitjacket (the first and last one I ever saw) until a doctor examined him.

He was later sectioned under the Mental Health Act and detained at the hospital. A few days later, after an all-points bulletin had been distributed to other forces nationally asking if anyone knew of him, we got a reply from the police in Belfast. A mental hospital there had reported him as an escapee. It would appear that he'd somehow escaped through a broken window leaving the remains of his fingers on the glass and then, having jumped about thirty feet into a river, he just disappeared and it was assumed that he had drowned. To my knowledge it was never ascertained why he was in Ireland in the first place, how and why he ended up in the mental hospital and then how he managed to get back to England and his mum and dad's house.

Just imagine your only son disappearing for eight years and then, just when you've accepted that he's probably dead, he turns up again. The joy, thanks and elation of that happening must have been incredible. Add to that the cruelty of having to lose him again in the space of a few hours and in such horrifying circumstances. Our hearts went out to them and all of us, including the boss, chucked in a few bob and bought some flowers for poor old mum.

It made us feel a bit better for having done so and when the inspector delivered them we hoped that it would somehow help for them to know that someone showed some sympathy for their stressful predicament.

CHAPTER TEN

A Dog's Life

Sheffield is sometimes called Little Rome because it is built on seven hills. Lots of the older people who lived in Darnall in particular said that the 'seven airs' met in High Hazels Park in Darnall and used to say how beneficial to your health it was to take in the 'seven airs'. Two of these hills were contained within the Attercliffe police division. One was the Manor and the other Wincobank and both invoke memories for different reasons.

The small police sub-station on City Road at Manor Top was our divisional boundary office and was manned by two officers from our division and also two officers from the neighbouring Woodseats division. The beats were vast, and with so many people to police we usually used a push-bike to get around on in the early 1960s, and then later came the

Ariel Leader motorbikes and the Morris Minor Panda cars.

I remember one of my early shifts at Manor Top as if it was yesterday. It was 1962 and the coldest winter on record and there was deep snow well into May. It was so cold that before I left my lodgings to go to work I put my pyjamas on underneath my uniform. All the lads did the same and some of them even wore a pair of their wife's tights, which had come into fashion as a result of the mini-skirt trend. I couldn't have worn them to save my life; I'd rather have frozen to death.

In those days Manor Top became a magnet for taxi drivers on nights because opposite Elm Tree Bakery was a small parade of shops near the bus shelters. Outside one of these shops was a newly installed machine which could dispense tea, coffee, hot chocolate and soup for six old pennies per cup, or two and a half pence as it would be today. This wonderful, newfangled contraption was the first that anyone in Sheffield had ever seen and people, including our lads, queued up for a drink and the novelty factor. We thought this was very modern and up to date then and very high-tech.

Working up there on afters or nights was always extremely busy and it's a wonder that our pocketbooks didn't catch fire as we dealt with so many differing incidents, it was non-stop with drunks, fights and domestic quarrels. When I worked up there or down The Cliffe I never wore a wristwatch, preferring instead an unbreakable plastic pocket watch, which saved the expense of a new watch or strap being replaced after damaging it in the many fights and scuffles that we were involved in.

The Wincobank Hill area was far less populated than Manor Top and thus tended to be a bit quieter. Whether on foot, bike or in a car I loved being on top of this hill and near to the c.2,500-year-old Romano-British fort which overlooked the Roman fort and temple site at Templeborough. As dawn came up in the summer months I could see across the Don Valley to Tinsley, Brinsworth, Catcliffe, Treeton and Whiston; and my mind would wander back to the time when the majority of these places would have been tiny hamlets.

Brinsworth housed the civilian population from the Roman fort at the side of the River Don, what a sight it must have been then. If I'd been on Wincobank Hill with a pair of binoculars in the year AD 937, I may have been witness to one of the biggest and most brutal battles that ever took place in England: the Battle of Brunanburh, mentioned in the *Anglo-Saxon Chronicle*.

The Battle may have been fought in the areas between Tinsley, Catcliffe, Brinsworth and Whiston and would have involved many thousands of men. In the blue corner was King Constantine of Scotland who had got a large army together consisting of the Irish, Celts and Vikings. Their dream of taking over England was to be put to the test by

A Dog's Life

King Athelstan in the red corner. King Athelstan was the grandson of King Alfred the Great and was the most powerful ruler in England since the Romans had left our shores several hundred years before.

Both kings had large armies, but King Athelstan won with a knockout in probably the tenth round, well done England. I love history, although I hated it at school and as a metal detectorist of many years I would love to find the battle site.

A lot of people would have been killed that day including, perhaps, some of the tribal kings and I often wonder whether it is possible that if ten tribal kings were slain this could have been corrupted over the years from 'ten slain' to Tinsley, a possible place of burial for the ten kings that may have been slain in battle. This, I know, is all conjecture and possibly fanciful but, nevertheless, one day some eminent historian may prove it to be correct or otherwise.

The old police push-bikes were very heavy and cumbersome but at least if you were attending an incident going downhill then you got there quicker. However, the opposite applied when you had to push your bike uphill. On this occasion I was travelling down Prince of Wales Road to deal with a job on the lower Manor so freewheeled fast for about a mile, chuckling to myself at the same time.

A couple of weeks prior to this I was working Manor Top and my counterpart from Woodseats Division, PC George 'Spud' Turner, was working his beat on the opposite side of the road to me. It was about 4am and it was windy and drizzling with rain and so we were both wearing our capes to keep dry.

'Race you to the Rex,' said Spud, and we both jumped on our iron horses and set off down Mansfield Road towards the Rex Cinema about a mile away. It was all downhill and at 4am there was no one about to witness our childish behaviour. Heads down and feet off the pedals, we were going like bullets down the steep hill and Spud was leading by about half a wheel. Just as we were passing the cemetery I heard some loud, muffled cursing and turned to look at Spud on my left. The wind must have got under his cape which was now over his face and head. He had one hand on a handlebar trying to steer and the other hand clawing at the cape, trying to remove it from his face so that he could see where he was going.

I was laughing even before poor old Spud lost control of the bike and crashed into the cemetery wall. Luckily he wasn't hurt, apart from his pride, but his front wheel was as bent as a corkscrew. I don't know how the damage was explained away to his sergeant but old Spud 'hadn't come down on the up train', so he'd find some excuse.

So that's why I was chuckling as I freewheeled down Prince of Wales Road, thinking about Spud lying in a crumpled heap on the floor, still cursing under his cape, which was still over his head when he landed.

Someone had rung the nick reporting a lady throwing things out of the window of a second-floor flat including a small table, so would we investigate. When I arrived at the scene all was quiet and I spoke to a neighbour. The flats were fairly new so the families in them hadn't had time to get to know each other very well and it was thought that the lady concerned lived there alone.

The flat door was opened by an old lady of about eighty, who had a small white poodle at her side. As I explained to her why I was there I bent down to pat the dog which, oddly enough, was wet through. The old lady looked to be in a state of oblivion-like trance, with no conversation and no expression on her face, just blankness. She moved aside to let me into the house which looked clean and tidy and she just sat on the settee watching a small black-and-white television (no colour then).

Helmet off, I sat at the table trying to make conversation but got nowhere. I had to assume that she wasn't deaf, as the sound coming from the television wasn't that loud. There were pictures on the table and sideboard of the lady with a man that I assumed to be her husband and no longer with us, but there were no pictures of any children. The front window was wide open and on the ground below could be seen the stuff, including the small table, that she'd thrown out.

I was in a dilemma as to what to do next, no damage had been done but I just couldn't leave her like that and so I did what I always do in a situation where I need to think and mashed us a cuppa tea. Having passed the lady hers I took mine to the table and sat down again. After a couple of minutes she got up and walked down the hallway followed by her dog and a short while later she came and sat down again and watched the television. I thought I could hear a dog whimper but thought nothing of it until it did it again, and then again. Funny, I'll bet he's got shut in somewhere and so I thought I'd better let him out.

Opening all the doors revealed nothing, but I could still hear whimpering and then I remembered hearing the toilet flush earlier, so it was obviously in the bathroom. Opening the door I got a shock; there in the toilet bowl was the poor little poodle trying to climb out. Retrieving him from the toilet, I took him back into the living room just in time to see the lady throw the cups out of the window. As I went to close the window she went back down the hall and two minutes later came back dressed only in a nightie and she sat down to watch television again.

The poor old woman had obviously lost the plot and needed help. Sending for an ambulance was no good as she wasn't hurt and I daren't leave her in case she leaped through the window. What a mess. Opening the window again revealed a few people below obviously awaiting the next event and, thankfully, two of the ladies agreed to sit with her while I went to the telephone box 200 yards away.

When I outlined the circumstances to the office sergeant he said that it required a DAO (Duly Authorised Officer) to attend but, it being Sunday afternoon, I would have to wait at the house until one was sent for, which could be a while – great. The DAO would assess the lady's mental condition and needs and deal with it from there.

Back at the house, one of the ladies had left to go to work but I was glad of both the company and presence of the other lady, Joan. Things were forming a pattern now and the poor little poodle started the sequence of events. The poor thing would shiver as if knowing what was about to happen and then off they both went to the loo. The lady would then come back without him, which was my cue to rescue the dog again. By the time I got back she had opened the window and thrown something out; anything small like a fork or a spoon. Back down the hall again she reappeared fully clothed, partly clothed or in a nightdress, you never knew which.

One hour went by and then two. After three hours Joan and I were shattered and the poor dog looked like a drowned rat and a bit 'flushed'. My shift finished at 3pm and by the time the young lady from mental health arrived it was about 5pm and I was starving hungry.

In the house the DAO spoke to the lady, who didn't reply, and then she witnessed for herself what Joan and I'd seen about a dozen times over the past four hours and she quietly beckoned me to one side. 'I'm fairly new to all this – do you think the lady has a mental problem?' she asked. After waiting four hours for an expert, I couldn't believe my ears and just slowly shook my head in disbelief. The DAO wanted a second opinion and another hour passed before an older and more experienced chap came out to see us and dealt with the situation.

For ages afterwards when I heard a dog whimper I thought about the poor little poodle. Fancy, every half an hour being stuffed down the toilet and having it flushed on you. I had to laugh about it, but it must have been a nightmare and the expression 'barking mad' took on a different meaning.

Joan, the good neighbour, took in the dog and I was later told that the poor lady was placed into a home caring for people with mental health problems. Over the years we, all of us bobbies, dealt with older people wandering about, usually during the night. A lot of them had lost their loved ones and, for some reason, ladies in particular, would be found wandering the streets in their night attire, whilst men were usually dressed and trying to find their old place of work which they'd retired from many years before.

We don't always realise that people are lonely and it has always been important to me to pass the time of day with people young and old who I come in contact with. Often you will be told that you are the only person that the elderly person has spoken to in the last few days. Being on the beat allowed us to talk to anybody, old or young, and get to know them and keep the lines of communication open. We got to know people and, even in the city, we were familiar with communities and looked out for them; it was just an integral part of the job which we did as a matter of course. Unfortunately, with the advent of police cars, this personal contact has all but been forgotten. If you are in a police car, you often ride straight past the people who need you to just stop and chat for five minutes and make them feel that their life is a little richer and that they are cared about. I believe that this is an extremely important aspect of being a bobby, but in today's police force I am very sad that there isn't the time or resources to allow this to happen.

A very good friend and ex-colleague of mine, George Sweeting, the local Wentworth bobby, ended up in a similar way to the old lady and, unfortunately, at a fairly young age. He was a lovely man, well liked and loved by the community. He was involved in all aspects of country life and had a family who cared for him. But it was sad to see, and my heart went out to his family, as his slow deterioration led him to believe that he was still a beat bobby in Wentworth.

It is a sad fact that great pressure is put on families of people with these sorts of problems and they have a difficult time dealing with this and seeing their loved ones decline. For these reasons I would like to dedicate this chapter to them, and especially my old friend George.

CHAPTER ELEVEN

Permission Granted

Bloody hell fire, that bugger's shifting, an accident waiting to happen!

It was bang on 9.05am on a lovely spring day and, as the lollipop lady wasn't well, I'd just finished taking the kids across the road to school on Hartley Brook Road. A few minutes earlier and he could have easily knocked down a child or, for that matter, me.

Grabbing what is now the old-fashioned cork crash helmet, I banged it on quickly and fired up the 250cc Ariel Leader motorbike, not very fast I know, but it was all we had then.

He was in my sights now as I sped after him and I had to get him before he got to the busy Barnsley Road, half a mile in front of me. You could tell that there was no way he was going to stop and my priority was to reach the busy junction ahead before he did.

With a feeling of great relief I just managed to get there first and I jumped off the bike and stopped the flow of traffic in time, thus preventing a serious accident. As predicted, he went straight through the junction without even slowing down and I was, once more, chasing him.

The road ahead was long and straight for perhaps a mile, probably my only chance to stop him – but how? I couldn't summon help by using the big Bakelite phone on the bike whilst I was riding, which meant that I was on my own and it was almost impossible to stop anything on just the bike anyway. The road that we were now on was fairly quiet, but we were only a couple of minutes away from the dual carriageway on Halifax Road, one of the major routes into the city and always busy. Quick decisions were needed in order to avert a serious road accident from happening.

I managed to overtake him and rode about 150 yards beyond him, swiftly putting the bike on its stand as I stopped. As I turned I could see him coming straight at me and my blue trousers were starting to turn brown. Like all bobbies, I've been in many a scary situation and this, I can assure you, was one of them.

His eyes were wild and his coat was lathered up big-style and a broken piece of rope was round his neck with the loose end flying in all directions as he galloped towards me.

Milking cows, castrating pigs and helping sheep to lamb were second nature to me but I knew absolutely nothing at all about horses.

The sight of cars whizzing up and down the busy main road sixty to seventy yards away meant that I had to try something drastic to stop him ploughing into the cars ahead, and I had to quickly galvanise myself into action.

Roy Rogers and John Wayne would certainly not have approved as I grabbed the rope, which was tied round the horse's neck, thinking that I could maybe stop or slow his gallop. As an ex-blacksmith I was big and strong and as I flew up in the air I realized, too late, that I wasn't strong enough. I know what you're thinking and you're absolutely right. The words idiot, nutter, plonker and thick pillock were the ones that I used to describe myself as I was being thrown about like a piece of confetti. The power of this large stallion amazed me.

Not daring to let go and frightened to hang on made me thankful of the crash helmet that I was still wearing. At that time I weighed in at nearly seventeen stone and it was probably that, coupled with his fast gallop over perhaps three miles that slowed the horse down as we got to the junction. He came right down to a leisurely trot which, thankfully, gave the car drivers ample time to stop.

When I let go of the rope, I seemed to have lost all feeling in my arms and legs and I was quivering like a jelly. As we all know, hindsight is the best sight of all and without a doubt I could have been accidentally killed. Split second decisions can cost lives but also save lives and all a policeman can do is what he thinks is right at the time, without the benefit of hindsight. There is absolutely no doubt whatsoever in my mind that on that occasion people and the horse would almost certainly have been killed had it not been for taking a split second decision.

By this time Road Traffic, who had been alerted, arrived at the scene in the Zephyr Zodiac patrol car and controlled the traffic whilst, luckily, the stallion trotted up a nearby lane. What I thought was odd, though, was the fact that he seemed to have both direction and purpose. He seemed to know where he was going and you could see him visibly relaxing.

What happened next is something that I will never forget and, to me, it was mind-blowing. I jumped in the car with the traffic lads and we slowly followed the horse up the narrow road and saw him sniff the air and start neighing. We were now in fairly open countryside and his pace slowed right down and you could sense that something was about to happen.

At a point in the road the horse stopped at the side of a field with a banking about five feet high, on top of which was a wooden fence. What was he doing? Getting out of the patrol car I could see him prancing on his back legs and neighing like a good 'un. A few seconds later a mare and her foal showed themselves through the fence and then all three were showing excitement in a big way.

A chap arrived in a Land-Rover and got out looking at the frothed-up stallion. 'What are you doing back here, lad?' he said quietly as he patted the horse's flank. He went on to explain that he'd reluctantly sold the stallion the day before to someone about four miles away, near Ecclesfield, and he'd just had a phone call telling him that the horse had broken out of its enclosure.

'How did he find his way back?' I asked.

'I often rode him down there and I'll bet I can tell you which roads he used to get back home,' he replied. He told me which roads he would have come back on and, as you have rightly guessed, he was bang on.

The traffic lads and I had seen many nasty things, but when the chap led the stallion into the field to join his family we were enthralled. They were obviously relieved and pleased to see each other after their separation. It was one of the most moving things we'd ever seen and each of us had a tear in our eye as we watched their obvious affection for each other. The man's last words to us as we were leaving were: 'I can't really afford to keep him, but I'll take Joe his money back later today and keep him here where he is happy.'

*

It isn't often that you get a happy ending in the job that we were in and so we were chuffed to bits. Funny job, ours; one minute I was taking the kids across the road to school and then ten minutes later I was like Lester Piggott flying over Beeches Brook in the Grand National. What next? We never knew.

It was shortly after this incident that I borrowed a car and took Christine (my girlfriend) and my mum and dad to Filey for the day to get some sunshine. About two months before this, Dad had been trapped in a roof fall down the pit and he was lucky to have escaped with just several broken ribs. For weeks he was in agony and the near escape had unnerved him a bit, especially so as that was the second time that it had happened to him. Working half a mile underground was a hazardous job, but there weren't any other options then in the area that we lived in. Mum and Dad loved Filey, as did a lot more people who had got there before us.

The deckchair man on the cobbled landing was busy and doing a brisk trade, which wasn't surprising on such a lovely day. There were hundreds of people on the beach but we finally managed to find a spot near Filey Brigg and set up the chairs for a few hours.

Looking around me, I decided to play 'spot the coal miner'. An easy enough game to play, as their skin was as white as the driven snow because they saw less sun than most people, working as they did in the bowels of the earth. There was, however, another clue and that was the blue scars on their backs, sometimes referred to as 'tiger marks'. When lumps of coal fell on them whilst they were hewing it would split the skin open and leave the black coal-dust in the wound. When this healed it left a dark-blue mark on their backs just like the ink from a tattoo. The older the miner, the more hits he'd taken and some older men, like Dad, were covered in them.

We had a great day out apart from when a wasp stung Dad on his bottom lip as he was eating an ice cream. The bigger his lip got, the more we were laughing, we just couldn't help it. It must have hurt because it swelled up so much that his lip looked like a small plate. We were laughing all the way home but, always being up for a laugh himself, he took it in his stride and did his best to laugh with us, even when I told him to have less lip.

I was as nervous as a kitten after I'd dropped Mum and Dad back home in Darfield. Christine and I were going to get engaged and, while I still had the borrowed car for a few hours, we'd arranged to pick up her parents, Mabel and Albert, and take them for a meal. For me, as a traditionalist, it had to be done right, and I was going to ask Albert's permission to marry his daughter.

One of the lads had told me about a pub called The Moss Brook at Eckington in Derbyshire where they served 'chicken in a basket'. I'd never heard of such a thing, but all the 'in' people were visiting the pub, which was becoming famous for this brand new idea. It sounded daft to me, fancy running out of plates.

The meal went OK I but I thought it was a barmy idea and especially when they brought the sweet list, whoever came up with the idea of frying a banana and covering it in syrup must have lost their marbles, it looked revolting. The pub itself, the service and the atmosphere were fantastic and Christine and I often call in when we are in that area and wish at times that it was nearer to where we live so that we could call in more often.

Christine and I held hands under the table when I asked Albert for his daughter's hand in marriage. The poor man nearly choked on his banana fritter, but he said yes as he shook my hand. It was then my turn to choke as I had to pay the bill and kiss Mabel, my future mother-in-law. I've made plenty of mistakes in my life but this wasn't one of them and I wouldn't swap Christine for the world.

In those days, believe it or not, getting married to a policeman wasn't as easy as it is today. A written application had to be made to the Chief Constable for permission to marry. Details of the girl concerned had to be given in full, including her religion, nationality, old schools and places of work. All this instigated enquiries to be made as to the girl's suitability to marry a policeman. Criminal records were checked and enquiries made at local shops in the area where she lived to ascertain if she owed any money or if she was troublesome. When all these enquiries had been satisfied permission to marry would be given.

At that time very few policemen other than the ones in higher ranks could afford to live in a private house, the wages quite simply could not sustain a mortgage. Most lived in police-owned houses which were in small clusters within the division itself. Assuming that you had been left money and could afford to buy a house of your own, you were still required to live within one mile of the divisional boundary and a further restriction barred you from living on business or licensed premises, which I suppose was understandable.

As our division was in the industrial heartland of the city we had very few choices of where to live, so chose to hang on for a while in case the regulations were relaxed sometime in the future.

The Tinsley viaduct was steadily taking shape having been started in 1965, and was due to be opened in March 1968. At that point the M1 motorway, which was also under construction, would go at least as far as Thorpe Hesley which, as the crow flies, would be only two miles beyond the divisional boundary. If I could get permission to live there I'd be as happy as a pig in muck, back in what was then the countryside.

Eventually the Tinsley viaduct opened on, I think, 24 March 1968 and people came from miles around to watch the first vehicles crossing it. The M1 was also opened to Thorpe Hesley and then after that it was extended in stages, finishing in Leeds. This pushed house prices up in Thorpe Hesley and so, for our first year of marriage, we lived in rented accommodation until we could save enough money for a deposit.

Permission had been given for us to marry,[1] and then to buy a house in Thorpe Hesley. In 1970 we bought a new three-bedroomed detached house for £3,900 with a mortgage of £31 per month. When we moved into our new house all we had was a portable wireless, but no TV, our entertainment for the first year was playing cards. My mum and dad bought us a fridge, Christine's mum and dad bought us a carpet, her sister, Barbara, gave us her old settee and we bought a bed, and we happily lived on hanky-panky and baked beans.

---

[1] I was in the Bridge Inn in Darfield, just after I had asked Christine's dad's permission to marry her, when I bumped into an old-timer who was a good friend of my dad's. He was a right character and full of fun. 'Is it right that tha's getting married, lad?' 'Yes, Mr Ship, I am.' Mr Ship was a lovely old man of about eighty, born and bred in Darfield. He always wore a big flat cap and had a twinkle in his eye. 'Let me gi' thee some advice young 'un. Get thissen a decent-sized jam jar and a packet of dried peas.' 'What for, Mr Ship?' I asked in amazement. 'For when tha gets married, lad,' he replied. What the hell was he on about, I thought, but then he continued. 'Every time thy as a bit of "that there", put a dried pea in thi jam jar. In six months' time it will be full.' He was looking very serious and I hung on every word and then I respectfully asked him what for. 'Every time you have sex after tha's been married for six months tek a dried pea out of the jar, an' I'll bet tha never empties it.' With that he shuffled away, laughing his head off. After forty-three years of marriage I'll leave it to your imagination as to whether the jar is empty or not!

CHAPTER TWELVE

All in a Day's Work

Afters was my least favourite shift and more so as I was working Firth Park on foot patrol. There was nothing wrong with Firth Park, but if I finished later than 11pm it would mean that I would miss my bus connections home and would then face a four-mile walk back to my lodgings.

A stroll down through Longley Park brought me to a small group of young lads who were playing marbles. Nearby and near some huts a group of girls were playing hopscotch and some others were skipping with a long rope and chanting songs at the same time.

It was nice to listen to the birds singing in the trees and see people lying on the grass in the sunshine. We were lucky in Sheffield in that the council had provided many parks in which everyone could play and relax during the summer months and the sound of laughter was every-where.

The sight of the lads playing marbles was all that I needed to see and I walked over to them. Before I knew it, the helmet came off and I was on my knees playing marbles myself, much to the glee of the kids.

'Can you skip, Mr Policeman?' a girl shouted and, on turn-ing round, I could see the other girls giggling to themselves.

'I don't think so, but I'll give it a go,' I replied. I couldn't get the hang of it and they all laughed when I got the rope round my ankles and fell over. Hopscotch was a different matter though and, with a bit more practice, I am sure I could have become a professional.

After a great half an hour with the kids I was as dry as the Gobi Desert and ready for a cuppa. As I left, the kids were waving goodbye and the lads were telling me to get some practice in ready for the next time we met up. They'd enjoyed it just as much as I had and, anyway, they were right; it must have been about eight years since my last marble tournament at school, and I needed to practice.

Audrey Sykes was one of the nicest ladies you could ever wish to meet and she must have looked through the window of the outdoor swimming baths where she worked and seen me playing with the kids in the park. Knowing that I was on my way she'd already mashed and I was presented with a mug of tea, which she knew I preferred to one of them daft little cups. Audrey was the jack of all trades at the baths: ticket lady, changing-room attendant, lifeguard, waitress in the café, all at the same time. A real workhorse.

The pool was busy and I could hear people in it shouting my name, which surprised me somewhat. When I looked into the pool I could see all my neighbours from Darnall, Bill and Eileen Downes and their daughter and son, Sharron and Vaughan. They were all swimming happily and having a lovely time. It was Eileen's birthday, so they had decided to get together with Audrey (her sister), and her niece, Beverley, and have a pool party for a change. How I wished that I was in there with them, but after supping my tea, I was off again on the beat.

My next point was the phone box at the bottom of Firvale and just as I got there the sergeant pulled up in the Hillman Husky. I was where I was supposed to be and he signed my pocketbook to that effect. About five minutes after he'd left a motorist pulled up to tell me about a traffic accident at the roundabout on Bellhouse Road three-quarters of a mile away.

Thanking the chap for telling me, I stopped a car heading in the direction of the accident and commandeered a lift to the scene. When I arrived, I could see a small car on my side of the roundabout but facing the wrong way to which he should be facing. Not many yards away and facing in the correct direction was another car. The driver of this car was being spoken to by the Road Traffic lads, who had obviously got to the scene before me. Neither car looked to be damaged, apart from the one nearest to me, which had a broken windscreen.

It was rush hour and traffic had built up around the round-about and no one could move one way or the other. The traffic lads were there before me so it was their job to deal with, along with any help that I could give. The driver's door on the car nearest to me was wide open and a large chap was sitting in the passenger seat, but where was the driver? I'd marked out the car's position in the road by drawing around it with a piece of stone that I'd found and the car could now be moved out of the way.

'Where's the driver, mate?' I shouted through the open door. Cars and buses were trying to get past and, because of the noise, I didn't hear him reply. Shouting again produced no response and I had to get back to controlling the traffic. So much needs to be dealt with and quickly in a situation like this and, as I looked at him as I worked the traffic, I was cursing him under my breath for not answering. A couple of minutes later there was total gridlock and I angrily ran to the passenger door and nearly pulled it off its hinges as I wrenched it open.

'I've asked you three times, now where is the driver?' Still no reply. So I grabbed his shoulder and, as I did so, he slid towards me and I got a shock – the poor man was dead.

I couldn't believe it, and felt terrible. In those days there were no seat belts and he must have lurched forwards in his seat, on impact, and broken the windscreen with his head. The only sign of injury to the man was a tiny spot of blood in the middle of his forehead. Later at the mortuary it was discovered that a windscreen-wiper blade had been driven into his skull and brain and then, as he lurched backwards in his seat, the blade had removed itself.

The driver of the car was eventually traced and charged with driving whilst disqualified, with no insurance or driving licence, leaving the scene of an accident and causing death by dangerous driving. The dead passenger was his own father.

It was Road Traffic who dealt with the accident so I was glad that I didn't have the job of telling the man's wife that he was dead and that her husband had been killed by their son. I'm sorry I can't tell you what happened to the son in court, but he must have pleaded guilty or I would have been called as a witness and then I would have known the result.

Luckily for me I finished the last of my 'punishment beats' shift at 11pm and caught the bus back down to The Cliffe, hoping that I would get my connection with the other bus back to Darnall. It was the usual banter on the bus when people had had a drink or two. 'Do you know what time it is, Hocciffer?' was a common one, and when I replied with a chuckle, 'Time you bought a watch, mate,' everyone laughed.

The atmosphere was great and I loved being part of it. I'd learned early on in my career that if you made people laugh it often helped to stop any animosity that may be coming in your direction.

In my mind's eye I could see and smell the meat-and-potato pie that I knew Mrs Proctor was making for my supper. It would be between two plates and all I had to do was heat it up in the oven for half and hour or so, as she would be in bed by the time I got back. I couldn't wait for that pie with some Henderson's Relish on it, which we didn't have in Barnsley.

As I got near to the police box at the bottom of Staniforth Road, near to where I would catch the bus back to Darnall, I could hear and see a right commotion. It was coming from one of the roughest and toughest pubs, not only in Sheffield, but also in Yorkshire, the notorious and infamous Dog and Partridge. Because of the time that it had taken me to get from Firth Park to here by bus, I could see that some of the night-shift lads were outside the pub, as was the Black Maria or prison van.

Fights were fairly common at the pub and we all got used to them. Some were worse than others, like this one appeared to be, but most lasted just a few minutes and involved only a few people.

Even though I was now off duty and the night shift were in attendance, walking past was not an option, so I crossed the road to see if my help was required. A few prisoners were in the back of the van and, looking at their injuries, it seemed to me that they were the losers. One of our lads told me that the fight had started between two women and then had spread out from there. It was now all under control and I was just about to leave and get the bus when there was a shout from within the pub, 'Someone's just stabbed the landlord.' At the same time a youth ran out of the door brandishing a knife. He looked straight at me and kept coming. In the nick of time I grabbed my heavy, folded-up cape from my left shoulder and, just as he got to me, I whacked it round the hand that was carrying the knife. The knife dropped to the floor. As he bent down to pick it up the night-shift lad caught him with a punch to the head and down he went, out for the count. He was cuffed and thrown into the van with the other balmpots, and off they drove to the charge office. The landlord went to hospital with a superficial wound and wasn't badly hurt. As for me, I'd missed the bus and had to walk home, arriving just in time to see the white dot on the old TV disappear into the middle of the pink screen, as the BBC service shut down for the night.

For some reason I can't stand gravy, but Henderson's Relish on a pie is fantastic and I woofed it down in minutes, I was that hungry. That night I slept like a log and, instead of dreaming about the nasty things that we got involved in, I dreamed about marbles, skipping and hopscotch, and the lads were right, I must practise marbles more.

Pub fights are sometimes what I, as a Yorkshireman, like to call 'sommat and nowt' (something and nothing) and if dealt with in a certain way, a situation can easily be defused. Fifty years ago we worked our beat alone and not in pairs as today, and this meant that tact and a bit of gumption was often a better ploy to use than direct confrontation.

The Staniforth Arms on Staniforth Road was a reasonably well-kept pub, but had a few big drinkers as customers. One evening I got a call to attend the pub to deal with a scrap that was taking place. As I walked in through the front door I could see that half a dozen of the regulars were brawling with each other, but apart from fat lips, black eyes and cut faces, none looked seriously hurt.

Past experiences had taught me what was likely, but by no means certain, to happen next, and in this case it did. At the sight of me in police uniform, everyone stopped for a second – I had to be quick.

'Okay, lads, you all look as if you've had enough, now pack it in.'

'It's nowt to do wi thee, —— off,' and Mr Gob-on-a-Stick then slowly moved towards me, saying, 'Let me get at him, I'll knock his bleeding head off.'

At this point I had become the enemy and instead of

them fighting each other I was now the focus of their collective attention. His former enemies now grabbed his arms and held him back and it was at this point that I knew it was him who had kicked it all off in the first place and, more importantly, that things were going according to plan – mine, not theirs – time for Act Two.

'In less than two minutes, half the force will be here to assist me. Do you wish to make a complaint, landlord?' I asked in an authoritative voice. They all looked at him.

'There's a few broken glasses, officer, that's all. No, normally they're good lads.' And you could see the relief on their faces.

'Thank you, landlord. Now if anyone wants a scrap with me, here I am' (the secret was then to pause for a few seconds but NOT too many). I continued, 'If not, get off home now, before I change my mind and lock you all up, and that includes you, Mr Mouth Almighty,' nodding to the instigator. It was funny to see. His pals were leaving in all directions as he looked around him, and he realised that he was now on his own. One step forward by me was all it took and he too legged it.

'Beers in, wits out and never sup owt that's stronger than you' was my motto. None of them were what I would call fighting lads, but if they had been fighters it could have turned nastier. My timing and judgement of the incident had to be just right.

There was, of course, no back-up, we were on our own in those days and if I'd gone barging into them with all guns blazing, things would have turned out differently. It required good timing, a few white lies and allowing an escape route for them with a bit of dignity to ensure that no more blows were struck, no bones broken and letting the landlord be the apparent boss in order for it to have worked and it also ensured good police and public relations.

It had all started off when Mr Gob-on-a-Stick had lost all his money at cards and had accused his mates of cheating. I knew that the next day, after work, they'd all be pals again and back to see the landlord of the pub in the hope that he hadn't barred them.

The whole incident had lasted no more than five minutes from start to finish, and it meant that the pub was now empty, leaving the poor landlord on his own, what a shame! I've always been a sociable bloke and so I joined him for some light refreshment which, on afters, was a rarity. He was obviously grateful for the help and after a few beers he got his son to drive me back to the police station to ring off duty. A short stagger back to my lodgings and bed took me to the end of a good shift.

Over the following weeks I bumped into all the lads concerned in the scrap individually, sometimes over a beer or whilst I was working the beat. They were all extremely apologetic and grateful for the fact that they had not been locked up that night and neither had they been barred from the pub. Sod's Law being what it is, the last person I saw was Mr Mighty Mouth who came looking for me to apologise and I had to smile when he said to me, 'I think I might have lost that fight the other night anyway, do you?' Looking down at him I said, 'Possibly so.' He was about five-foot-six tall and quite slim; in fact there looked to be more fat on a cold chip than there was on him and I'm sure that if he'd flexed his muscles his vest would have fallen off. As I've said before, 'When beer's in, wits are out.'

CHAPTER THIRTEEN

The Thinner Blue Line

'Hello 49, hello 49. Go immediately to Shepcote Lane where a train has crashed.'

'Roger, over and out,' I replied and was off.

The Ariel Leader motorbikes had no blue lights and I had to be careful as I sped towards the scene a couple of miles away. Like the bike, my mind was racing, the operator who'd given me the message must have somehow got it wrong – a train crash on Shepcote Lane? I knew the road very well, but train lines, no chance, as far as I was concerned, so I slowed the bike down to a more normal speed.

As I got to the Greenland Road junction with Shepcote Lane I could see nothing but standing traffic, so there had to be something going off somewhere. All the steelworks were at the end of a shift, so traffic was chaotic to say the least, and the dual carriageway was solid. None of the emergency services would be able to get through, so I had to somehow and quickly establish what was happening ahead.

Threading the bike through the cars was too slow, so I used the pavement instead. Half a mile further on, just past Tinsley Wire Industries, was a concrete bridge above the road and hanging down from it was a large railway engine with a carriage trailing behind it on the grass banking, what a sight. People were out of their cars and standing about near to the engine, and, as far as I could see, I was the only person there from the emergency services. Where do you begin?

Luckily the engine and carriage had no one in them, and it had landed on the pavement and road below. A couple of cars had just managed to stop in time as the engine landed on the road in front of them. It was a miracle that no one was hurt.

Assistance arrived having gained access down the opposite carriageway and, after the traffic had been sorted out, the road was closed and the railway police dealt with what could well have been a catastrophe.

Unbeknownst to me, the concrete bridge carried a railway line that was part of the huge Tinsley railway marshalling yards, which weren't under our jurisdiction. The road was closed for a couple of days in order to retrieve the engine and carriage using special equipment. I never knew what caused the problem but assumed that someone had pulled a wrong lever or something, causing 'Ivor the Engine' to push 'Thomas the Tank Engine' over the edge and off the rails.

A couple of years after this incident, and again in Shepcote Lane, the British Steel Corporation had gone on strike for some reason and prior to this some government boffin had devised a new method of crowd control. It was called 'trudge and wedge' and over a few days some of us bigger lads had been versed in the noble art of trudging and wedging. This involved twenty officers linking arms with each man on either side of him and then clasping your own hands together in front of your chest, thus forming a human fence similar to chain-link fencing.

The idea was to push back a crowd and, in order to achieve this end, all of us on command had to step forward one pace with our left foot and then bring our right leg forward and in line with the other foot. On each command you pushed the crowd backwards by one pace. How easy is that? No riot shields, no body armour, no riot helmets with visors, no collapsible batons, no CS gas and no taser guns, just a fifteen-inch-long piece of wood which we couldn't get at because we had to clasp our hands together.

In those days we weren't aware of the above products, so we couldn't complain that we hadn't got them, but even so questions were asked.

'Sir, what happens if they chuck bricks at us?'

'Just shrug it off, lad,' came the reply.

'Sir, what happens if we need our truncheons?'

'Don't break the line, you'll not need them. Okay?'

It was only a training exercise anyway, so it was forgotten about until a few months later and the strike at Shepcote Lane happened.

We were accustomed to peaceful marches and the odd strike and, to be honest, no one was interested in who was right or who was wrong but on this occasion things were different. When we arrived we could see that some of the strikers were getting agitated and directing their anger towards us, even though we were only observing from across the dual carriageway and some distance from them. The agitators were in a smallish group, away from the main body of strikers, and if they worked in the steelworks I'll eat my hat. You could see photographers, presumably the press, urging them on to have a go at us and for no reason whatsoever.

As they crossed the road towards us, throwing stones at the same time, the command was given to 'link arms and don't break the line'. We were like sitting ducks, and we couldn't even defend ourselves, what a farce.

Bricks and stones were flying in all directions and a burly bloke ran straight at me and kicked me on the shin and then deliberately gozzed (spat) at me, which hit me on the mouth. At the same time the lad next to me must have been hit with a brick or something and blood was pouring from his nose and mouth.

It's very, very rare that I lose my rag and get angry, but I'd had enough of this holding hands and arms malarkey. No one spits at me without retaliation, and I think that you'd be the same. B ——— s to 'hold the line', now it's my turn and I put three of them down within probably one minute. Some of our lads had done the same as me and there wasn't a truncheon in sight. While some of the mobsters were being handcuffed and arrested, the rest had legged it to wherever they had come from, which was definitely not Sheffield.

The strikers themselves didn't even know who they were and I believe that only one of those locked up came from within Yorkshire.

If we hadn't broken the line we would have been seriously hurt I'm sure, and if I ever find the jobsworth who invented trudge and wedge, I'd shove his trudge, followed by his wedge, right up his jacksy.

I never heard of it being used again and the policemen of today certainly need the right equipment to deal with incidents like that and, just like anyone else, we have the right to defend ourselves. Sorry for getting uptight but politicians, jobsworths, do-gooders, health and safety, all know best on how to deal with incidents like these but they're never there at the sharp end of the stick, which infuriates me, and the expression, 'if you can't do it yourself, teach it' comes to mind.

That night, after tea at my digs, I went for a pint at the Conservative Club on Darnall Terminus; I wasn't into politics, but I used to go to the club for several reasons. Harold and Maureen were the stewards and they made a good team. You could also get a game of crib and dominoes, which I loved, but the main interest to me were the early bar customers who, like me, loved a laugh and banter.

Maureen was behind the bar when I walked in and I ordered a pint. 'You'll know Maureen. How long does a chicken keep in a freezer?' I asked. Very few people had fridges then, never mind freezers, but I knew that the club had just recently acquired one.

'Now you're asking something – I don't know,' said Maureen, 'I'll look in the manual,' and off she went. A couple of minutes later she came back with the manual and was reading it on the bar.

'What make is the freezer?'

'I'm not sure, love,' I replied.

'Do you know how many stars it has, then?'

'Sorry, Maureen, no I don't,' and the more she read the manual the more rattled she got. Five minutes later she suddenly said, 'Three months, yes that's it, three months.'

'That can't be right, Maureen,' I said.

'Why not?'

'My landlady put one in last night and it was dead this morning.'

Harold and all the lads were in stitches with laughing, especially when Maureen chased me round the club brandishing a snooker cue, and for the second time that day I found myself in danger, but this time I deserved it. It had been an exhausting day and after a couple of pints and a few laughs I went back to my digs wondering what the next day would bring and slept like a log.

A little while after this I was working a large beat with the use of a Morris Minor Panda car when, at about 1.45am, I spotted an old car on the grass verge at the side of one of the major roads leading into the city. At that time in the morning something had to be wrong, so I stopped in the darkness to investigate.

No one was in the car but when I walked around the other side of it, I was surprised to see an empty wheelchair, of all things. The bonnet of the car was hot and the keys were in the ignition, which told me that it hadn't been there that long, so what was happening? Searching around near the car in the darkness showed up nothing except the lights of a lorry trundling towards me on the main road and as it got nearer I saw a sight that I will never forget.

Standing near to the edge of the road was a young lady on

crutches. As the lorry got nearer she started to walk laboriously towards it and the poor woman's intentions were obvious. The twenty-five-yard distance between us seemed like a mile as I sped towards her, grabbing and pulling her to one side at the last second, before she jumped in front of the lorry.

As I helped her back to her feet I could tell that both her legs were encased within metal callipers and the poor lass was partially paralysed. For a few seconds there was silence and then I got it in the neck for interfering with her object-ive. There were no tears and she was quite calm and matter-of-fact about what she had wished to do.

We walked back to the car and, when she got in, she had to press a lever or something near her knees and manually bend her legs in order to gain access to the car, which had been specially adapted to be used by her hands only.

She had been born in Cardiff and then moved to Sheffield with her family when she was ten years old. Getting her to talk and open up to me was hard work, but this was her story. She had, if I can remember rightly, polio when she was young and as a result she had to use crutches all her life. As she'd grown older all her girlfriends had boyfriends, most of whom later became husbands and obviously this was very upsetting for her and another cross for her to bear. She desperately wanted to have a relationship with a boy and in the absence of one she rebelled against authority and the world in general. A couple of years later she met a man in a similar plight and physical condition as she herself was in and at last they fell in love and married. A few months after this she found out that she was pregnant and both of them were ecstatic with joy. Six months into her pregnancy her husband suddenly died and the trauma brought on by this also caused her to lose the baby. So within a year she had gone from sublime happiness to the depths of despair and loneliness and, without her husband and baby, life was not worth living. She couldn't take any more and that is when I found her.

Her story took over an hour to coax out of her and I realised then that I was in a very privileged and important position. The position of trust and the receipt of information that, until now, she had been unable to impart to anyone.

It was now 3am and snap time back at the nick but, if I left her, I knew what she would do. Having gained her trust to some degree, I realised that the only way to stop her doing anything daft was to stick by her, but how could I do that when I was working?

'Follow me back to the station and I'll make us both a cuppa, okay?' and she agreed much to my relief.

The on-duty sergeant was Harold Singleton, or Snuffy as we called him. He was a good old guy and, after I'd explained the scenario to him, he agreed to cover my beat, which at that time in the morning would be quite quiet anyway.

We sat outside the station with a cuppa and shared a ham sandwich and a banana and I also gave her the car keys back which I'd managed to take from her when we arrived at the station just in case she decided to drive off.

A question here and a bit of encouragement there, along with the odd fag, encouraged her to open up even more. She was highly intelligent and the knocks that she'd suffered in the jungle of life had made her very shrewd and wise, but also cynical of the organisations that had advised her on different things.

'How can anyone advise me on how to deal with the problems that I have if they themselves have never been there?' she said. My heart went out to her, as I'm sure yours would, and I had to agree with her observations and sentiments, but at least I'd got her talking about it. Even before the end of the shift at 7am I knew what I had to do and did it.

After a knock on the door I heard the key turn in the lock and when the door opened, I was greeted with a kiss from Christine, my wife of a few months. It must have been a surprise to greet your husband at 7.30 in the morning, accompanied by a young woman whom you'd never seen before, but knowing me as she did Christine knew that there would be a good reason for it, so she promptly put the kettle on. Whilst I was out of the room I knew that the lady herself would have to explain to Christine the reason for her presence in our new home, thus making her open up, to now two people instead of none at all.

Christine is and always has been a diamond and she is also a good listener. I could hear the story I had heard previously being repeated to my wife, including how and why we had both met, and then Christine said, 'Try not to worry too much; you are safe now and not on your own.' On hearing that I went to bed for a few hours knowing that the young lady was in good hands.

She stayed with us for quite a while and slept on the settee. Christine and I spent hours and hours just talking and listening to her and discussing her problems, and each new day brought slight changes. On the third day she even managed a smile, which was nice for us both to see. Her concerns for herself and her attendant problems were slowly subsiding, but she couldn't believe that a policeman and his wife would bother to help her. In truth, she didn't want to believe that two perfect strangers could offer her refuge, help and a bed because it didn't fit in with her opinion of people in authority or people in general.

After a couple of weeks she left, after grudgingly saying thanks for stopping her suicide bid. Over the next couple of years she would just turn up, sometimes staying a night or two and sometimes not. We chose not to pry into her private life, knowing that if she wanted to tell us, then she would. When she came to see us it was usually Christine that she wanted to see and talk to and she always said that Christine had a calming influence on her which helped her to cope.

Her visits got less frequent and we both knew that she would now survive. About three years after we first met, we got invited to her second wedding. We felt very privileged to be there and, as requested, no one knew the background to our relationship.

I have seen her a couple of times since that day and she has children of her own. The last time I saw her she seemed extremely happy.

NB: There is only one person in the world other than Christine and me who, on reading this, will recognise who I am talking about. If by any chance it is you, I know that your dark days are, thankfully, at last behind you, and both Christine and myself wish you all the very best and, as you know, you are always welcome.

CHAPTER FOURTEEN

What a Load of Tripe

I was 'gypping' and retching even before I switched on the lights, the smell was absolutely revolting. A little while earlier I'd been asked to check out some premises near to the city boundary, where an alarm bell had been heard ringing by a man out walking his dog.

Sunday, on afters, was usually quiet on this, a motorbike beat, and at 4pm it was my first call to a job. Avoiding the potholes in the lane leading to the remote premises, I could see on approach that one of the doors to the building was opening and closing in the breeze, and that this was the probable reason for the alarm bell ringing.

There was no apparent sign of a forced entry to either the door or the door jamb, but it was better to be safe than sorry, so I walked into the largish building, very gingerly.

The smell was dreadful and as I opened an internal door and switched on the lights it got worse, which is why I was gypping. After a slow walk round the premises I found that nothing appeared to have been disturbed and the door had probably not been properly closed when the staff left.

The fresh air smelled sweet as I got back to the bike to ring the station, requesting that the owner attend and secure the premises. There was no one about so I lit up and waited, knowing what would happen next. Sure enough, about twenty minutes later the owner arrived and once more I had to go in and check the premises with him.

'Sorry for the inconvenience, Officer, it'll be young Ivor rushing off to catch his bus home, he's forgot to lock up properly before.'

'Don't worry about it, it's a shame to have to call you out,' I said, 'but I have to ask, how can you stand the smell working in there?'

'You soon get used to it and it tastes delicious. Which is your favourite? Honeycomb, elder, cow heel, thick seam or chick-lings and bag?' he asked, as he held out a large carrier bag full of tripe and laughed at the same time. He could tell from my face that I didn't fancy it.

I love liver and kidney and, when I was younger, I've eaten many an hedgehog, but for some reason whelks, oysters and tripe in particular I can't stand the sight of it. This factory got it straight from the abattoir and then they put it through all sorts of processes. It was a smelly job for the people who worked there but I suppose they got used to it, the whole of the premises smelt of it which was why I was gypping.

The lads back at the nick loved it when the alarm went off at the tripe factory and when I went in at snap time they knew that the owner, as usual, would have sent to the station a large bag of goodies to share. What a load of tripe. Verbal earache was the order of the day for me, as I had to put up with the abuse from my mates.

'From Barnsley and you don't like tripe, I can't believe it,' said big Albert.

'Come and get some of this honeycomb darn de,' said Les, dangling the tripe under my nose.

I was glad to get out of the nick and back on duty, but every dog has his day and I was chuckling at the thought of getting my own back.

The chuckling didn't last long, as I received an urgent call to attend an address in the area of the city where the CID lads were planning to raid a house. They'd also called on the other motorbike officer within the division to attend as well, but not the Hillman Husky patrol car. 'How odd,' I thought, 'why us?' It was a strange request, maybe we were needed to chase another motorbike or something, but I'd have to wait and find out when I got there.

When I arrived at the appointed meeting place at the end

of a quiet cul-de-sac I could see three CID cars nearby. Everybody in those days, including criminals, knew a CID car a mile away. They were Morris Minor cars and nearly all D registration (1965 model) and they were all a mucky brown colour, the colour that private owners wouldn't be seen dead in, so the force must have bought them cheap.

My mate, PC Tony Garnett, was just getting off his motorbike when I pulled up and did the same. Tony was a great guy and senior to me, and when the CID man in charge came to talk to us it was Tony that he addressed.

'Right, Garnett, and you,' nodding towards me, 'follow me.' We crept to the corner of a house from where he pointed to another house further down and on the opposite side of the road. We then retreated back to where we had first met.

'Why have you sent for us, sir?' asked Tony.

'We've had a tip-off that inside that house is a dangerous criminal who is armed with a gun. Okay?'

'But what do you want us for, sir?'

'To break the door open and go in first.'

'Right, sir, but why do you want us to go in first?'

'Because you two have got crash helmets on and we haven't!'

I couldn't believe what I was hearing, and poor old Tony stood there with his mouth open at first.

'Sir, with all due respect, wouldn't it be better to call for a police dog and handler and send the dog in after the door's opened?'

'Good idea, Garnett, radio for one to be sent out now, go on lad, quick.'

After a while PC Alan Radley, who was one of the first police dog handlers in Sheffield, turned up with his dog Tito. Alan was a big strong bobby and a brilliant bloke and he crept to the side of the door with Tito on a long lead. After knocking on the door it was opened by a man who froze when he saw the police dog, and a few minutes later he was arrested by the CID lads for something or other, but as far as I'm aware they never found a gun.

The following morning saw me up bright and early and I was picked up by a mate of mine, John Longbottom, who I later worked with in CID. John kept a few hens near his mum's house at Swallownest and he was talking about getting a few pigs as well. We were going to see my uncle Jack at his farm in Howbrook, near High Green, for two reasons. About ten days before he'd asked me to go and help him castrate some pigs, and the second reason was so that John could pick his brains about how to keep a few pigs himself.

On our arrival, Aunty Mary cooked us a great breakfast of fresh farm eggs and home-cured bacon, which was delicious. In those days all farmers cured their own bacon. A whole side of pork was placed on a stone slab and packed in salt.

After two weeks the salt was removed and then, after the side had been washed, it was hung to dry, in a dry atmosphere. After a week you could slice off the amount of bacon that you required and it would remain fit to eat for about a year after being cured. A meal fit for a king.

The pigs were normally castrated after they were six weeks old, while they were still small enough to be manhandled but, because I'd been busy, they were now nearly eight weeks old and had grown a bit bigger. It was my job to lift them up and hold them in between my knees, belly forward, so that Uncle Jack could do his bit. If I held them steady it didn't take long, a quick rub round with Dettol and a squeeze of the finger and thumb, before the use of a razor blade, a dab of iodine after the removal of the testicles and that was it, next one. They squealed a bit, but when I think about it so would I if someone did that to me. Thank goodness that this operation is done in a more humane way these days. Having said that, they were as right as rain again after a couple of minutes, but there were more pigs to do than I thought.

After our job was done Aunty Mary gave us some bacon to take home with us and we just got back to Sheffield in time to start work at 3pm.

Back at the station, it was my turn to work the telephone switchboard while Barbara Greaves, our usual telephonist, had her half-hour break. When the phone rang it was the telephonist's job to put them through to the extension that they required, by pulling out the plug from one socket and placing it into another one that had the extension number written on it. Each plug had a long cable which would reach from one hole to the other. It made the whole thing look like a gigantic puzzle of wires, which I found a nightmare.

I was all fingers and thumbs at it and once got the superintendent out of bed by mistake when someone wanted to be put through to the CID office instead. There were wires going in all directions and I'll bet that's where the expression 'crossed wires' comes from. Barbara, and Sheila Adams, another telephonist, were really good at their job, and if we were on nights they'd often tell us where the sergeant was so that we could have another ten minutes snap time.

By the time that the lads arrived back at the station at meal time, I'd got a big cast-iron frying pan on the go and I was ready for them.

'That bacon smells great, any spare?' said Les.

'Had any tripe lately?' said Albert. Ignoring them, I placed the big frying pan in the middle of the canteen table.

'Help yourselves, lads, it's all fresh from the farm today.'

Within two minutes it was all gone and even Inspector Jacques, who'd put me on punishment beat and sent me to London, had some.

'Delicious,' said one.

'Fantastic,' said another.

'That bacon was great, but what were those round things?' the inspector asked.

'Balls, sir, pigs' balls or sweetbreads, as some people call them.' For a few seconds there was deadly silence and then big Albert piped up. 'A dar telling me av just etten pigs' bleeding knackers, Martyn?' The inspector turned a funny colour and started to gyp, John Longbottom was laughing his head off and Les just sat there with his mouth open in disbelief. As usual I couldn't talk for laughing, and Tony Garnet said, 'There were nowt wrong with them son, but I couldn't have eaten em if you'd told me what they were.'

Looking at big Albert, I was ready to run. 'Fancy, coming from Sheffield and not eating sweetbreads,' I said.

'Fair play to de kid, next time da goes, get some more, will da. They were all right, dem.'

'Were they better than that tripe you eat, Albert?' And we all started laughing, apart from the boss who'd gone to the toilet.

Hell, I hope he's not been sick or I'll be on punishment beat again, I thought.

Back on the bike, I was casually riding along Holywell Road in Brightside when suddenly, in front of me, I saw a large lorry laden with heavy steel bars emerge from Limpsfield

Road, which was a very steep and quiet residential road. It shot straight out of the junction at high speed, narrowly missing the car which was travelling in front of me and at the same time it caught the front wing of a car travelling in the opposite direction, which spun the car around like a spinning top. All this, as you can imagine, happened in a split second and, after hitting the car, the lorry went into a low wall, which lifted it into the air and then, about twenty yards further along, it landed on one of the railway tracks carrying all the main railway traffic in and out of the city.

People were climbing out of their cars now as I leaped off the bike to assess the situation. Priorities, priorities, priorities. The lorry was just settling in a cloud of dust and I could see that the heavy steel bars had been dislodged and shot forward onto the railway line, and the cab of the lorry had been sheared off completely.

The driver, who was clearly beyond all help, would have to wait, as would the car driver who was only slightly injured. My priority was to avoid a potential catastrophe in the form of a train crash.

I grabbed the telephone handset on the bike to contact police control and at the same time stopped the traffic in both directions. At my request an ambulance and fire engine were sent for (we would certainly need cutting gear) and also the British Transport Police were urgently asked to close the line. For all I knew the line could be electrified and so, at that point, the poor driver, or what was left of him, would have to stay where he was.

'Can I have a word, Officer?' said a man.

'Later, mate, I've enough on my plate already.' And I went to check on the car driver but, thankfully, he was okay.

All the emergency services had arrived by now, along with the Railway Police who had somehow managed to close the lines and power sources.

'Can I have a word please?' He was there again, there's always one at every incident and when critical decisions are being made you can do without it.

Things were calming down a bit now and I wasn't looking forward to the messy job of dealing with the driver of the lorry, and at this momment laddo came again. 'Can I have a word, please?' And he looked very sheepish indeed.

'What's up?' I asked

'I'm the driver of that lorry there,' he said, and pointed to the mangled lorry on the rail track. I was speechless and again looked at the lorry.

'Are you telling me that you've got out of that lorry alive?' I asked incredulously.

'No, I was never in it.'

'What the hell do you mean?'

'I've just come home for my dinner and live at the top of that hill [Limpsfield Road].'

'And?'

'I parked the lorry pointing downhill and the load must have been too heavy for the handbrake to cope with. I got a shock when I went for the lorry and it wasn't there.'

I nearly kissed him knowing that I hadn't to deal with what would have been a really messy body, but decided against it.

Eventually it was all sorted out and the driver was reported for failing to set his handbrake properly.

They say that no two days are the same but on our job no two hours were the same, and you never knew what the next job would bring. That night I finished on time and bumped into Tony back at the nick.

'Keep your crash helmet on, son,' said Tony laughingly.

'Why?'

'There's a crazed gunman on the loose in London and they want us on the job first, because we've got crash helmets.' And he shook his head in total disbelief at what we'd been asked to do the night before.

When I look back, it's hard to believe that sometimes decisions as daft as that one were made, but I can assure you that it's true.

NB: If you look at the wall opposite the bottom of Limpsfield Road, you can still see the repaired area where the lorry hit it before landing on the railway track.

CHAPTER FIFTEEN

Happy Christmas

Christmas was always a busy time, whichever beat you were on, especially on a motorbike. Regular drinkers imbibed more than normal, and ended up either fighting or just simply falling down and staying where they'd fallen because they couldn't get up again. Either way there was a lot of hassle and arrests and, in the main, 'found drunks' were locked up for their own safety. Non-regular drinkers were the same, but because they weren't used to drink they tended to want a fight or fell down sooner. The only difference between then and now is that you didn't get binge drinkers as such, and it was very rare to see a woman drunk. Unlike today, shorts like whisky or gin were about fifty per cent more expensive than beer, and lager was virtually unheard of; and a lot of the pubs in Sheffield only had a licence to sell beer.

At times Christmas could be great fun and, apart from the police-station pantomime for all the bobbies and local kids, which I loved, my festivities usually started with playing Father Christmas. Schools were usually the first to ask me, followed by Sunday Schools and junior youth clubs. Being single and having the time meant that I could also enjoy it myself. One of the schools that I played Santa at was what I think today would be classed, maybe, as a special-needs school and, because some of the kids were unruly and aggressive, no one would take on the job. It was certainly different and I suffered kicks, scratches, beard-pulling, and once had a bucket of water thrown over me, but those little kids were going to see Father Christmas just like all the other kids were, as far as I was concerned, so it didn't matter.

I was working Manor Top one night around Christmas time when I walked out of the sub-station at 11.05pm. People were just leaving the pubs and the three working-men's clubs on City Road when I could hear shouting coming from nearby. 'He's going to kill somebody.' Coming towards me, doing between five and ten miles per hour, was a car containing a man at the wheel with his head bent down.

As I went to stop him, I could see that he was driving erratically and, at the last minute, I had to jump to one side before he ran into me. You could see that the people were right about him killing someone. He didn't know where he was or what day it was either. As I ran alongside him, his head was on the steering wheel, but I couldn't open his door to get at his keys. He was obviously not going to stop and I'm sure he didn't even know how to, and it was only a matter of time before he hit someone or something. Luckily he was driving very slowly and, along with myself, other men were trying to stop the car as well. As I smashed the glass in the driver's door with my metal police lamp, a chap on the other side of the car managed to break the glass in the passenger-side door with a house brick and, luckily, he was able to lean in and grab the handbrake and stop the car.

There were no breathalysers then and, after the inspector certified him as drunk, I took him to the charge office on Water Lane where he had to be seen by a police surgeon.

The charge office was always busy at night, mainly with drunks. When the sergeant-in-charge shouted or looked at you, you then went to the counter with your prisoner and gave your reason for the arrest. He would then ask the prisoner his details such as name and address. It was like a madhouse and the old sergeant took no nonsense, even we were scared of him.

A young bobby from West Bar had arrested a man as 'found drunk' and took him to the counter. 'Name,' shouted the sergeant. The man answered by giving the name of a very famous statesman. At that point the old sergeant slapped him across the face. 'Don't be smart with me, lad.

Get over there.' Several minutes later, he sent for him again. 'Right, lad, I'll ask you again. What's your name?' He hesitated, but answered and gave him the same famous statesman's name again, at the same time he got another clout.

My prisoner was fast asleep and as I waited I thought to myself how daft drunks were by trying to be smart, when will they learn? Just then an old bobby from Hillsborough Division came through the door with another 'found drunk' and looked at the queue. He looked at the man with sore ears and shouted, 'Nah then Winston are tha drunk again?'

'Is that his real name?' asked the sergeant. When the bobby nodded, he went on to say, 'Sorry lad, but you should have said. Come on, I'll find you a soft bed for the night.' And he was led away to the cells. I bet the poor man cursed his parents for giving him his famous name. I don't suppose for a minute that they ever thought he would be in trouble with the law.

As usual, I saw the funny side of it and couldn't stop laughing. The chap wasn't hurt, but in those days things were different and I'll bet Winston thought twice about getting drunk again.

The police surgeon examined my prisoner and took two blood samples, one for testing by the forensic science laboratory and the other for the prisoner to have an independent check if he so wished. When the tests came back they were the highest blood-alcohol figures ever recorded in Sheffield and it made a big story in the *Sheffield Star* when the case went to court.

He was trying to find his way home from a meeting of Alcoholics Anonymous and his surname was synonymous with a well-known Irish drink. I can't remember what happened at court, but whatever punishment was meted out, it was well deserved – as the crowd said, he could have easily killed someone.

A few nights after this I was working the beat down The Cliffe and watching the coming and goings as the pubs turned out. Closing time in those days was 10.30pm and drinking-up time 10.40pm. Because the many pubs in the area were disgorging so many people, I was standing near the police box at the bottom of Staniforth Road in case I needed to phone for assistance.

It was a happy atmosphere with lots of laughter and I was having the usual banter with people. Some of the women were a teeny bit tipsy and you knew what the comments were going to be. 'Is that a tit on your head, Hoccifer, or is your head pointed?' or 'Can I have a feel of your truncheon?' And then just as I was awaiting the next one, which was 'I've always wanted to kiss a copper,' someone shouted, 'I've always wanted to knock a copper's f—g head off.'

Turning round, I could see two young lads of about

nineteen or twenty with their fists up and shadow-boxing like boxers do before a fight. I could also see that they'd had a pint or two and were wanting to show off. Here we go again, I thought.

I was just about to speak when the woman I'd just been listening to hit one of the lads over the head with an umbrella. The umbrella bent and wasn't heavy enough to hurt him and he pushed her backwards into the outside of the police box. All this took about a second and I decided that I didn't like Mr Gobshite and that a night in the cells would calm him down a bit.

'That's my wife tha's shoved, and that's mi mate tha's slagged off.' And then as he hit him you could hear his nose break.

'Coppers haven't got any mates,' the lad said in a muffled voice.

'This one has, pal!' and he clipped him again.

It was Bob and his mate Keith who were now chasing after the other lad, who was legging it down the road. I'd had a run-in with Bob and Keith a few months before, but we finished up pals. I was just being introduced to his wife (the umbrella lady), who until now I'd never met before, when the phone in the police box rang.

'Don't worry about these two,' said Keith, who by now had collared the other lad. 'We'll deal with them, a dip in t'canal will cool 'em down.'

On answering the phone, the sergeant instructed me to attend a domestic in Shirland Lane, about 200 yards away. I turned and everyone had disappeared. What a funny carry-on, from someone wanting to feel my truncheon and then being threatened, followed by someone getting a broken nose, had taken at best two minutes and I'd not even moved or spoken.

I've said it before and I'll say it again. On that job you never knew what would happen next. Domestic disturbances or family squabbles could take many forms and all of us dealt with hundreds of them and, for whatever reason, they were all different.

Shirland Lane was lit by gas lamps then, so I used my torch to check the house numbers because it was that dark. The numbers told me that I had a fair lick of a walk to get to the house concerned and as I walked over the canal bridge I thought I heard a splash away to my right, but thought nothing of it.

As I neared the house I realised from the numbers that I'd been here before to another domestic. The usual man-and-wife domestic was when the husband had clipped his wife, but on my last visit to this address it was the other way round and the husband had copped for a shiner from his wife.

Walking up the entry to the rear of the house, I could hear the shouting and bawling – no wonder the neighbours had run to a payphone to ring for the police.

Jennifer was a big girl, about 6ft 1in and perhaps sixteen to seventeen stone in weight, and I remembered from the last time I saw her that she had the words LOVE and HATE tattooed across the knuckles of her hands, what a lovely lady she was. Dennis, her husband, was about 5ft 7in and weighed about eight stone wet through, and when you saw them walking down the street they looked like Little and Large. If it ever came to a scrap I'd want her on my side but not her husband.

'Serves you right, you drunken little bastard,' I heard her say as I arrived at the open back door, expecting to see Dennis with another shiner on its way. Poking my head round the corner of the open door, I could see Jennifer sitting at the far side of the kitchen table with her head bent forward and her chin resting on her folded arms, which were resting on the table.

'Who's sent for you bastards?' she politely asked. Being mindful of the possible hassle for the neighbours, I replied, 'No one, I could hear the racket two streets away. Where's Dennis?' Nodding towards the living room, she shouted, 'Dennis, bleeding coppers want you.' I could see that he was drunk as he staggered into the kitchen holding his head and I had to look twice before I could see why. I couldn't believe my eyes. Sticking straight up in the air and wobbling about as he staggered was, of all things, a carving knife, which was firmly stuck in the top of his head. Going to his aid I could see hardly any blood at all and closer examination revealed that the very thin blade had pierced the scalp only. On contact with the skull the blade had bent and got stuck under the scalp itself and he was perfectly okay after I removed it.

'How did that get there, Dennis?' I asked him. Quick as a flash, Marilyn Monroe spoke up, 'It fell off the top cupboard and landed on his head, didn't it, Dennis?'

'Er, it must have done, duck, I can't remember,' he answered.

'Why are you rowing with each other, anyway?' I asked.

'It's his birthday today,' replied Jennifer.

'Happy birthday, but why row?'

'We went out for a few beers to the Dog and Partridge,' she answered.

'And?'

'At 10pm I told him that I was off home to get ready,' she said.

'Ready, what do you mean?'

'I was going to surprise him with his birthday treat, but when he came in he was too drunk to do it, so I picked up the carv ...' Then she hesitated, 'Er, er, and that's when the knife fell out of the cupboard.'

During this time she had never moved from the table and suddenly said, 'I love him really,' and then jumped up from the chair and walked over to Dennis. My eyes nearly popped out of my head at what I saw next.

Jennifer, who I said earlier was a big girl, had told me half the truth, and it was at this point that I realised why she'd sat at the table with her chin in her hands. One of the lads later told me it's called frustration, and, as she jumped up to cross the kitchen, I had the fright of my life. She was wearing thick red lipstick, white high-heeled shoes and a see-through baby-doll nightie which fitted where it touched. It was a cold night and if I'd had to take my helmet off I'd have been spoiled for choice as to where to hang it.

I daren't face seeing anything below the hem of the nightie and, as I left, I shouted, 'Happy birthday, Dennis, I've closed the door!'

By the time it was all over, the streets had cleared of people and so I went back to the police box for a fag and to report back to the office sergeant at the main nick. Telling him the story about the knife wobbling about made him laugh, but when I told him what happened next, and with whom, he was almost hysterical. 'She looks awesome with her clothes on, and I wouldn't want to see her without any. Was Dennis okay?'

'She was dragging him towards the stairs when I left and he looked terrified, but I'm sure he'll survive.'

I was behind in checking the shops for break-ins, so did the ones at the bottom of Staniforth Road. The Butterfly Chinese takeaway was next to the canal and I could see several puddles of water on the pavement. I followed them up Staniforth Road for a while until they got smaller and then disappeared altogether. 'Funny, what's that all about?' I thought, but I did wonder!

At about 5.30am I bumped into Bob, who was on his way to start work at 6am. 'Thanks for your help last night, Bob,' I said.

'No problem, Martyn, but somehow they fell into t' canal. It's a good job me and Keith were there to get 'em out or they might have drowned!' and off he went, laughing.

I was still laughing and thinking about the night's events when I went to bed.

'Are you all right, Martyn?' It was Mrs Proctor shouting from downstairs.

'Why?'

'You're shouting in your sleep,' she answered. Then it dawned on me, I was having a nightmare and Jennifer, in her baby-doll's, was chasing me with a knife. Was I glad to wake up.

CHAPTER SIXTEEN

A Night at the Dogs

Days were okay and nights were even better, but for some reason afters, 3pm to 11pm, were not for me, which was daft really because I had to work them anyway. It was probably because I was courting Christine and if something happened towards the end of the shift, which it often did, it meant that I couldn't let her know that I was working late and I wouldn't see her either.

Starting at 3pm at Darnall sub-station on a nice sunny afternoon saw me in shirtsleeve order with my sleeves rolled up, ready for what the shift was going to throw at me, and I didn't have long to wait. Ten minutes after starting I was walking towards Darnall Terminus whistling the theme tune from Z Cars, a TV programme that had been on television for the last year, and hoping that today would be a quiet one.

A squeal of brakes and a bang twenty yards away woke me up and, at the same time, a small dog which was yelping shot past me. Lying on the floor a few yards from me was a motorcycle, with its rider also on the floor a few yards further on. So much for a quiet day.

Running to him, I could see that the poor lad was in a mess. There were no crash helmets then, which, in this case, wouldn't have mattered anyway, as his head appeared to be okay.

'He swerved to miss a dog and hit them railings,' said a passer-by as I bent down to see what was what.

'I've rung for an ambulance,' shouted Jim from the nearby café.

As I knelt down I could see what had probably happened. The bike had hit the railings, which had twisted the handlebar and brake lever round. As the rider flew over the handlebars on impact, the brake lever had ripped into the poor lad's lower stomach and disembowelled him. He was lying on his back and, miraculously, his intestines were all in a neat pile at the side of him, looking fairly intact.

As is human nature, a small crowd had now gathered and I heard a woman shout, 'I'm a first-aider, let me through.' She was fairly young and, when she saw the poor lad's guts, she promptly fainted and I was on my own again and wondering what was the best thing to do for the lad.

Theory is one thing, but putting it into practice is

another. First-aiders' prompt action can and does save lives, especially so with the kiss of life. None of us are doctors or nurses and can only do what we think is right in those critical moments before the proper medics arrive.

Keeping the lad calm wasn't easy and I tried to reassure him that he was okay. I sent for some towels from the café and carefully wrapped them around the intestines to keep them together, in the hope that it would reduce his shock level.

The ambulance arrived and praised me for my actions. In less than ten minutes it was all over, but the adrenalin coursing through my body made me shake. The poor girl who had fainted was being looked after in the café and I sat on the back step with her for about twenty minutes, supping a pot of sweet tea, with a fag until I, like her, came round a bit.

As I was covered in blood I went back to my digs to change and then back to the station where I was met by a new sergeant, the one that no one liked, who said, 'Have you done that accident report yet?'

'Not yet, Sergeant, I haven't had a chance.'

'Get on with it then.'

A little later I finished the report and passed it to him, getting a rollicking for not copying the details off the bike's tax disc.

'Attention to detail is more important than anything,' he

said. What a paperwork plonker – a man's life is at stake and that's all he's bothered about, a bloody tax disc.

Luckily the man pulled through and I later got a nice letter of appreciation from the hospital doctor. I was still seething with anger thinking about the thoughtless and heartless jumped-up sergeant as I went back to the Terminus to resume normal duties. All was quiet and at about 6.30pm I went in for my snap. My landlady's son, Jud, had dropped a crab off for his mum and with a drop of vinegar it went down a treat. Earlier on at the café Jim had passed me two pots of something that was new then. They were samples and had been given to him by a company rep to try out. Looking at the label told me that this new thing was called yoghurt and, to be fair, they tasted okay but I still preferred my banana.

After snap time I called into the youth club on Station Road. It was a popular club and always busy. Normally, giggling girls were on one side of the room and bashful boys on the other. The mouthier the boys were and the bigger the bubbles they made with their gum, the more the girls giggled.

One of the games they played was new to me and was called Spin the Bottle. The idea of the game was that the boys and girls sat in a circle on the floor and one of them would be in the middle. The person in the middle spun the bottle and whoever it was pointing to when it stopped spinning had to go into the middle and was kissed by the person who spun it. Of course, if the one in the middle fancied someone they would try their hardest to make the bottle stop at them. There was lots of giggling and daft comments and a lot of fun. As soon as the kids saw me they tried to rope me in and at that point I made a quick exit.

For my money, calling in to the youth club every so often was a good way of getting to know the kids, but more importantly, it was good for them to know that we were there for them should they ever need us.

My next port of call was the outlying Tinsley Park Golf Club, near High Hazel's park. Over the previous few weeks several cars had been broken into and items of high-value golfing equipment stolen. None of the cars had been damaged and it appeared that in all cases access to them had been gained with a key or something similar.

The offences had taken place at various times of the day, and the main suspects were from the nearby gypsy encampment. None of the local swap shops or second-hand shops had been offered the stolen goods, so someone had a possible outlet for them outside the city.

A quick quid here and a quick quid there was the gypsies, MO (method of operation) and they used to flit from site to site, which made our job more difficult still when trying to arrest them. Trying to serve a summons or an arrest warrant on them was impossible as they used so many different names to avoid detection.

One day I visited the camp with an arrest warrant for Shaun M, who we knew was on the camp, but we didn't know what he looked like. Trying to pin him down was tricky, no one was admitting to anything.

'Is Shaun M knocking about?' I'd ask.

'No, sir.'

'Never heard of him, sir.'

'Doesn't live here, sir.' Just what do you do?

As I was leaving the site with the warrant in my hand a chap in his fifties shouted, 'I think he's maybe dead, sir.' To which I replied as I held up the warrant, 'That's a shame, he's just won the Irish Lottery.'

At that point, three or four of the men turned to a chap of about forty and said, 'Shaun, you lucky bastard, you've won the lottery.' I arrested him in a flash.

No one wants to be arrested and it was part of their ploy to put us off from doing so by telling lies. It was our job to catch them, sometimes by playing them at their own game, and on my next visit to the site there was no malice shown towards me. It was all part of the game. Some you win, some you lose and I still laugh about it even today and wonder if Shaun had ever bought a lottery ticket.

By the time I got to the golf-club car park it was about an hour before dusk and I stood behind a tree to keep an eye on the remaining cars. Nothing happened until about thirty minutes later when a green minivan slowly circled the golf course as I hid further behind the trees in order not to be seen. Because of this I didn't see the occupants of the van and, when one minute later they drove off the car park, I was disappointed as I thought they may be the culprits. Ah well.

It wasn't until the last car had left the car park that I realised that the minivan had turned right instead of left and back to Darnall. Turning right would take him onto the golf course itself, so what was he up to?

The light was fading, but I followed some tyre tracks for about half a mile across what I think they call a fairway, and for good reason. Silhouetted against the night sky I saw the minivan parked unattended near a bunker. 'Must be poaching a rabbit or two,' I thought, but if that was me I'd have set my snares early in the morning instead of now.

As I approached the tiny van to check the tax disc, I could hear strange noises coming from within it and at the same time I could hear the springs on the van squeaking in a rhythmic sort of way. I didn't need to be a detective to realise what was happening and that whoever was in there wasn't interested in snaring rabbits either. Not wanting to disturb things, I didn't approach any closer and, just as I started to laugh to myself, the noise stopped. At this point I was about ten yards from the van when the back doors sprang open and I got a bit of a shock. What a sight, a middle-aged bloke, who was puffing and panting, climbed out of the back of the van, followed by, of all things, four greyhounds. The man had no clothes on and, as I first looked at him and then at the dogs, who were also puffing and panting, my mind went into overdrive. Surely not, never, no way, not with a dog – all went through my mind.

As I switched on my torch and started to walk towards them, the man nearly passed out with fright and the dogs began to bark. Luckily for me, like all greyhounds they were friendly enough and as I got to the van, to my surprise, a heavily built woman climbed out and threw a pair of jeans to the man.

I was almost dumbstruck, but I had to think of something to say fast. 'Sorry to have disturbed you both,' I said sheepishly; and then thought, why am I apologising? 'Next time don't use the golf course for mankin', okay?' I was off like a shot and shaking my head at what I'd just seen. How the hell could you get two people and four dogs into the back of a minivan in the first place? Then again, why would you want to anyway? Then, to cap it all, have sex with four dogs around you, no wonder the poor dogs were puffing and panting when they were allowed to get out, it must have been red hot in that van, in more ways than one.

For the next ten minutes I was laughing my head off at the thought of it all. One minute I was going to lock the poor chap up for bestiality and a few seconds later I was glad to leave the scene.

Telling the story back at the nick had the lads in stitches, especially when one of them said, 'What was his handicap?' Knowing nothing about golf meant that I didn't know what he meant at first, but after several comical and unprintable comments I worked it out.

By the time I'd finished and got to Christine's house, she was in bed, so I knocked on the back door of a local pub and had a laugh and a few beers with the landlord and landlady. I told them the tale and, when I mentioned a green minivan, the landlord pricked his ears up.

'Do you know her, Bill?' I said.

'No, I don't think so, but I know of her, I think. If it's the person I'm thinking about, she is supposed to have won a few grand on Littlewoods pools a few months ago and bought a minivan. She's no Diana Dors to look at, and rumour has it that since her win, she pays for men to have sex with her. Can you believe that?' he said.

'She was a big girl alright, even though I only saw her legs hanging out of the van, poor lass.'

A couple of weeks after this and yet more thefts from cars on the golf-club car park, something had to be done and we decided to stake it out in pairs. Sunday mornings were always busy at the golf club and PC Brian Wild and myself were up there for about 7.30am. Even though we wore civvy jackets, we were still aware that we might stand out a bit so took cover behind a hedge on one of the nearby allotments. We were prepared for a long wait, but within about twenty minutes we were watching a lad of about twenty prowling round the car park and looking through the windows of parked cars.

We could only see his head above the cars and when he moved his head from side to side to make sure no one was watching, we moved in. His head disappeared from view and, as we went to grab him, it came back up again in a second. No way had he had the time to do anything and our cover was blown. 'Damn', or words to that effect, I muttered to myself. A split second later we were on him and, unbelievably, he was carrying a full set of golf clubs in a bag. On seeing us he dropped them and started to run, but Brian got him and he was arrested.

Holding an arm each, we walked him back to the station and searched him. But there was nothing, no keys, screwdriver or anything, clean as a whistle. The lad was as calm as a cucumber and readily admitted that theft, along with the many others from the golf-club car park.

The CID lads were sent for and, while we were waiting, I asked him how he got into the cars without damaging them. One of our lads' cars was parked and locked outside the station. 'I can get into any car I want to, sir,' and he nodded to the car, 'watch.' Within a few seconds, even with Brian holding him, he'd opened the door. We searched him again, but it still revealed nothing and he even smiled as we scratched our heads.

When the CID lads arrived we explained our arrest to them and his actions with the car outside the nick. They were as intrigued as we were and, after searching him again, he did the same with the CID car. No wires, no tools, no keys, even the shape of his fingernails were checked and, after he'd done it a further three times, we all gave up. He was taken to the main police station at Attercliffe and apparently did the same to the cars there and it was never discovered how he did it, but he did.

No further stolen property was ever recovered and he was charged and bailed to appear at court; and, a few weeks later, I was back at the gypsy site with a warrant for his arrest for non-appearance at court.

'Not here, sir.'

'Never heard of him, sir.'

'He may be dead, sir.'

I had to laugh. I'd already won one, but this one I'd lost and I've never seen or heard of the lad since, but I'd still love to know how he did it.

CHAPTER SEVENTEEN

Spare a Thought

Many is the time that I wished I'd been a bobby in a small rural town or village, where you were likely to deal with far fewer incidents than in a city.

At Pannal Ash Training School at Harrogate there were policemen from fourteen different forces and, when periodically we all met up, we would chew the fat and exchange stories. The workload of some of the country force lads was far smaller than the city lads and I envied them in some respects as I was in a city force which had other advantages and sometimes disadvantages.

'PC 656 attend road accident at —— , where a child has been knocked down, ambulance on its way.'

Being human, these were the calls that we dreaded the most and as I started the car engine, I was saying a silent prayer for whoever was concerned. A minute later I was there and it was unfortunately obvious that the prayer had come too late and the little five-year-old boy was dead. The accident had happened on a fairly quiet cobbled road with very little traffic and the child had run straight in front of a slow-moving but heavy car, which had run right over him.

In the few minutes before the ambulance arrived there was a terrible silence. Both parents and the car driver were in deep shock and gently rocking to and fro on the chairs that someone had provided. I covered up the little body with a blanket from the car and then did nothing but become part of the awful silence brought on by the tragedy. Nothing I could say to the parents or driver of the car in that first two or three minutes before the arrival of the ambulance would have meant anything, they weren't in a fit state to listen.

It is only the people in the emergency services who would understand what I mean and most people don't realise the effect that dealing with these terrible situations can have on us. A feeling of complete and utter hopelessness, emptiness and despair pervades your whole being in the knowledge that you cannot alter things and make them better.

Some of the pain and strain of these incidents are, like the funny stories, vividly etched in your brain and that is why you can never forget them.

As the ambulance arrived, the two crewmen and myself exchanged knowing looks and I could see from their faces that, like me, they were fed up because it was too late to help.

The child's body was taken to the hospital and officially pronounced dead. It was early evening and, knowing that he would have to be taken to the mortuary in Nursery Street, I agreed to meet the ambulance there. There were no attendants on duty so I picked up the mortuary keys and met the ambulance lads as arranged. After giving me the documentation from the doctor, who had pronounced death, and the little body itself, they were gone, back on call.

Somehow I had to make him look as presentable as possible for when the poor parents had to formally identify their son. As I lifted his broken little body and placed it on a trolley the tears started to flow. I tried to clean him up a bit, but kept having to stop and dry my eyes. One side of his little face was badly damaged, so I laid his head on one side to stop his mum and dad seeing it. After covering him with a white sheet I wheeled him into a small chapel, used for just this situation.

Standing on my own outside the mortuary, I had a quiet five minutes with a fag and, I'm not embarrassed to say, a few more tears, knowing that the next bit would be the hardest.

Having picked mum and dad up I explained as tactfully and thoughtfully as I could what to expect at the mortuary. As I led them into the chapel they were in a trance-like state and my heart went out to them. I gently moved the sheet from the little lad's face and both mum and dad, under-standably, broke down. I stood back to give them some time together.

Two minutes turned to four as they were kissing him good-bye. They knew that he couldn't go back home with them, but they didn't want to leave him on his own. It was heart-wrenching for them and pitiful to see. Eight minutes soon turned into twelve, and then fifteen. Then, through all our tears, I managed to coax them away and back into the Panda car.

Just as I was pulling away from the mortuary with mum and dad I noticed smoke about twenty yards in front of me. Where was it coming from? Mum and dad were obviously in a traumatic state, so what should I do? I couldn't ignore it and I could see that it was getting worse.

Apologising to them, I jumped out of the car and ran the very short distance to the junction with Nursery Street and the Wicker. On my left was a shop and I could see smoke and a few flames inside the premises. I phoned 999 for the fire brigade and at the same time looked at the building again.

Lights could be seen shining through some curtains above the shop and I realised that it must be a flat or something; and that they were likely to become trapped up there.

There was no obvious door to the flat and so I raced round the back and, in the darkness, found a fire escape and a door at the top of it which I banged on very heavily. Luckily a bloke answered it and, when I told him what was up, he was out of there like a flash.

The fire brigade arrived along with a West Bar bobby, who I gave the mortuary keys to. At the same time I asked him to drop the keys back at the charge office where I'd picked them up from before meeting up with the ambulance crew at the mortuary.

My interests and involvement with the fire were now over as I had passed that responsibility to the fire brigade. My main concerns were for poor mum and dad, who'd had to deal with the most horrendous day of their lives and then, to cap it all, be witness to a fire while grieving for their son.

I apologised for the inconvenience but thankfully they understood and were okay about it. Back at the station I did the necessary paperwork and report and by the time I'd done it was about 2am.

The night-shift lads were busy so I had to walk the couple of miles back to my digs. At that time in the morning there was no one about and, as I turned into Staniforth Road, I saw a very large lorry pulling up at the side of the road. As the main headlamps were switched off I could see from the registration that it was a foreign lorry which, in those days, was a very rare sight on our roads. He was pulling up before I got round the corner and at that time of the morning I assumed he was lost. I was still about fifty yards from the lorry when I saw a man climb out of the cab. At first I thought it was a co-driver, until it dawned on me that the lorry was a left-hand drive.

'What's he up to?' I thought, and stood in a doorway to clock him (watch him). Walking round to my side of the lorry I saw him bend down and he appeared to be looking at the large front wheels. Still bent down, I saw him stretch out both his arms as if in exasperation and at the same time there was a loud bang and the poor chap went flying backwards, landing on his back in the middle of the road. He was clawing at his face with both hands and screaming in agony. As I ran to him he regained his feet and, still with his hands clutching at his face, he was staggering round in the road and screaming even louder.

Holding his shoulders, I tried to reassure him, saying 'Police, gendarme, politzi. You go hospital!' in the hope that he understood that he was going to be looked after and that he was at least safe. Quickly guiding him to the police box seventy yards away, I phoned for an ambulance and for Road Traffic to attend.

Gently removing his hands from his face, I could see that it was well bloodied and hundreds of pieces of black stuff were embedded in his face. These turned out to be pieces of rubber from one of the large tyres that had exploded in the poor bloke's face. He couldn't open his eyes, which were also impregnated with rubber, and he was in absolute agony, as well as being very frightened.

It would be a little while before the ambulance came and in those days most people smoked. The day had been a long one and I'd only got one fag left which I lit and placed in the driver's trembling hand. The brown nicotine stain on his finger and thumb had told me that he smoked (people didn't use tipped cigarettes as much in those days), and he mumbled something to me in a foreign language that I didn't understand.

When the ambulance crew turned up they whisked him off to the hospital and I left the Road Traffic lads to deal with the lorry.

By the time I got back to my lodgings I was physically and mentally drained, and I could have murdered a pint or two. To make matters worse, I was starving hungry and had no fags left. After making and eating a cheese sandwich, I sat on the settee with a pint pot of tea and started to ponder on the past few hours and the events involved.

The poor dead little boy and his grief-stricken parents will be in my mind for ever. The man in the flat was lucky to get out unscathed from the fire and a poor lorry driver was stuck in hospital in a foreign country not knowing anyone and without his family for support.

All these things made me think. Here I was whinging about being tired and hungry with no fags and no pint. Suddenly those things became totally unimportant, what right had I to feel sorry for myself? Absolutely none, and for a moment I felt ashamed of my selfish attitude. Amazingly, dealing with sad and nasty incidents like these also have an upside. The upside has made me realise that life in general is a bonus and the chance to live it to the full is, in my opinion, an opportunity that we should grasp with both hands.

The following day was my day off and I didn't surface until dinner time. The home-made steak-and-kidney pie, with sloppy peas, went down a treat and I wobbled down to the section station, I was that full. My enquiries had told me that the lorry driver was at the Royal Hospital near West Street, so I jumped on the 52 bus to go and visit him.

Documents had been found in the lorry by the Road Traffic Division and the owners, who were from Barcelona, had been informed of the situation. The middle-aged driver was also Spanish and when I met him, he looked like the invisible man with all the bandages. I wasn't surprised when the nurse told me that he'd lost the sight of both eyes, poor man. He must have recognised my voice and when I put twenty Park Drive into his hand, he shook my hand and kept saying something that to me sounded like 'grassy arse'. It made me feel better that I'd been to see him, in the knowledge that he would know that someone was there for him.

I enjoyed a few beers that night and won at crib, but I kept thinking about the poor chap who'd been blinded. The Road Traffic lads said that the tyres were inferior remoulds that had got too hot and simply blew apart, poor man. I visited him once more in hospital and the company that employed him had arranged for his repatriation the following day, along with the return of the lorry to Spain. I shook hands with the driver, but wasn't too happy because as I was leaving the hospital he kept shouting 'Grassy arse, grassy arse, grassy arse'. It was weeks later when I was relating the story to a mate of mine that I had to laugh when he said, 'You thick pillock, that means "thank you" in Spanish.' Being a Barnsley lad, the only foreign language I knew was Sheffield talk.

Along with the driver of the car that had run over the little boy, I later attended the funeral. I put on my white gloves and saluted the tiny coffin as it went by, as all of us in the force did in those days, as a sign of respect. I felt better that I'd been and the parents thanked me for doing so.

I'll never forget that sad and stressful day and it was one that made me envious of the quieter beats in the country. Not all days were like that one, thankfully, and every day brought something new; and sometimes they could be fun.

CHAPTER EIGHTEEN

The Northern General

I knew just the place. Even though I didn't work this side of the Division as often as the other, I'd still found quite a few cuppa-tea spots that I could call at, even on a lovely sunny Saturday afternoon.

Hospital food was supposedly poor, but it wasn't so in the staff canteen at the Northern General Hospital where I was now heading. The canteen was near to the old Accident and Emergency unit, which we were always being called out to, for various reasons. It was dead handy for the odd cuppa and I would always have a bit of banter with the girls who worked there, they were good fun.

I'd called in there a couple of months earlier when I was on a motorbike beat. I had a laugh and a joke with the girls and then got a call to attend a domestic disturbance. Firing up the bike, I was off, but as I went round a roundabout I wondered what was happening. The bike was clanking and rattling and I thought that the engine was falling out, until the sound stopped. The same thing happened at the next roundabout and then stopped again.

After dealing with a family squabble, I was off again and when the same thing happened again I stopped and checked the bike. I couldn't see anything wrong, and couldn't reckon it up, until I opened one of the panniers to get a report form. Both panniers had been filled with empty milk bottles and empty tin cans, and I realised that the canteen ladies had got their own back for my tormenting them earlier on. I hadn't seen them since then and as I turned into the hospital grounds I was laughing about that night.

Driving into the entrance from Barnsley Road I could see that a cricket match was taking place on the field. What a stroke of luck. At that time there was a petrol shortage and we'd been told to restrict our mileage to thirty miles per shift. It couldn't have worked out better for me, as I parked the Panda car facing the pitch. The sergeant's words were, 'Only drive if you have to' and so here I was, legally watching my favourite game; what a bonus and I'd have a cuppa in the canteen after the match.

I was secretly hoping that they were a man short, I'd have loved a bat, but both the doctors' team and the other team from Ecclesfield were full so I had to be content with watching.

It was good fun, but the doctors' team were fielding as if they'd all got broken legs. The umpire was witty and when one of the Ecclesfield team managed a boundary he shouted 'four', followed by 'ceps' (forceps) and everyone laughed. With one over to go, a giant of a lad came in to bat and was obviously going to give the ball some wellie, so I decided to stay. He swung his bat at the first three balls and missed, but if he'd connected they'd have landed in the River Thames. The next one was a tidy four, and at that point he'd got his eye in. The bowler came in for the fifth time and W. G. Grace strode down the pitch and gave it an absolutely thunderous great clout. We all watched as the ball rose high into the air and then it just kept on going and going. It was fantastic to see and we were all clapping as it started to come down, probably 100 yards away, what a beauty.

Our clapping got quieter and quieter as we watched where the ball was falling, and then with a loud bang it landed on my Panda car bonnet, bounced and smashed the windscreen. For a few seconds there was stunned silence and the batsman looked absolutely terrified as I walked towards him.

'Tha's made a right balls of that car, lad, but what a smashing hit.' At that point everyone relaxed, all except the poor batsman who thought he was going to get locked up with no 'bail'. It was an accident, and no one's fault, and while I was waiting for Road Traffic to bring me an exchange car I had a good laugh with the teams at snap time. The umpire was a youngish doctor and wittily said to me, 'What an arresting sight, I was stumped for words, Officer.' As we were chatting I saw the unmistakable black Zephyr Zodiac patrol car coming up the drive and my exchange Panda car was behind it being driven by a civilian.

As it got near to us I could see that the patrol car was being driven by PC Don Caley, a nice quiet reserved guy who later taught me on the police advanced driving course, which was fantastic. As I looked at the passenger, I realised that it could only be one man and that man was PC Charlie Lampard, another brilliant character who would do anything for a laugh. Today was no exception, and one of his tricks was to cut a table-tennis ball in half, paint a round dot on each one and then cup them into his eye sockets when he was a passenger in the police car, like now. He certainly looked comical as he got out of the car and the few kids that were knocking about looked at him in amazement.

It was good to have a bit of banter and a laugh with the doctors, something we weren't used to doing on afternoons, we were far too busy as a rule.

Ten minutes later I was back on the road again, and wishing that I could hit a cricket ball that far; it was certainly one of the biggest hits that I've ever seen.

'Aye, aye, what's up here,' I thought, as I saw a woman standing at the side of the road waving her arms in the air, about thirty yards in front of me. Pulling up, I could see that she was going frantic for some reason and was screaming hysterically, clutching at her chest, a sure sign of panic.

Trying to calm her down and tell me the problem was impossible, the poor woman couldn't get her words out and was having difficulty in breathing. It had to be really serious to be in a state like this and probably something that required urgent action. I desperately tried again to discover what was wrong, but she was just hysterical and the only way I knew to calm her down was to gently slap her across the cheek, which I did. Luckily it worked to some degree and she was mumbling as she pointed to the house behind us.

I ran through the open front door, not knowing what to expect, and turned right into the living room. There was nothing obvious in there and it was the same with the kitchen, so I ran upstairs. Bathroom: nothing; main bedroom: nothing; middle bedroom: the same; I must have missed something. The door to the box bedroom was open and I ran in.

There, lying on top of the covers, on a single bed, was the lifeless and completely naked body of a teenage girl of about seventeen years of age. She was on her back and in one hand was a photograph of a young man and I could also see three empty bottles which would have held tablets. Now I knew why the poor woman, obviously her mum, was hysterical.

No pulse, but she was still warm and I raced down to the car and rang for an ambulance to attend urgently. I also knew that we were about ten minutes' drive from the ambulance station and by the time they got here it would be too late so I had to take some immediate action.

As I ran back upstairs, I ripped off my tunic and my mind was racing. Better to try and fail than not to try at all. No time for textbooks, get on with it, lad. My own heart was thumping as I gently squeezed the girl's nostrils together with one hand and opened her mouth with the other, then I took in a gulp of air and exhaled into her mouth and then released the pressure on her nostrils. I did the same again and then again and again and again and just as I thought I'd failed there was a cough and a splutter and the girl started to breathe by herself. It was a moment that I will never forget and I was euphoric.

We were far from out of the woods, though and I knew that even though she was breathing again I somehow had to keep her awake because the overdose of tablets was doing its job. If the girl had been dead and without oxygen for more than five minutes, she could also suffer permanent brain damage.

Seconds counted and I shouted to the mother to bring a wet towel and quickly. I did this for two reasons, one to give her mother something to do and focus her mind, and secondly in the hope that the wet towel might come in handy. When she arrived I explained my predicament to her: 'Your daughter needs to stay awake and I need to manhandle her to keep her moving, okay?' The poor woman was beside herself with worry, which was understandable and, even though I felt awkward because the girl had no clothes on, I picked her up from the bed, stood her on her feet and held her up with both my arms around her for support. There was no time for niceties.

'What's her name, love?'

'Mary,' she replied.

'What's your name?'

'Sadie.'

'Sadie, put that cold towel on the back of her neck and then try to move her legs backwards and forwards as if she's walking.'

'Mary, Mary keep awake, don't go to sleep Mary, keep awake.' I kept shouting as we somehow shuffled around the little room together.

The drugs inside her had taken effect and she kept lapsing in and out of consciousness. I screamed at her: 'Mary! Mary! Keep awake Mary, keep awake. Wake up! Wake up!' and every time her body sagged and went unconscious again I got Sadie to splash cold water on her face in the hope that it would shock her into waking up a bit.

As the ambulance arrived, Mary was thankfully groaning a bit, which meant that at least she was still alive and with us.

Sadie was in my car as I escorted the ambulance at great

speed to the Northern General Hospital, which allowed the medics to do their job en route. They must have radioed ahead, as we were straight into the recovery room at Accident and Emergency where I gave a nurse the empty tablet bottles so that they knew what she had taken.

By this time poor old Sadie had calmed down a bit. Apparently young Mary had been ditched by her first boyfriend, hence the photograph in her hand. The hospital pumped out Mary's stomach contents but, according to the doctor, her survival would be touch-and-go.

There was nothing more that I could do and as usual I went for a fag. The doctor had been quite categorical about the fact that the prompt first aid had probably saved her life and I was glad when I phoned the day after and was told that Mary would be okay.

If I'd attended the incident in this day and age, that critical ten minutes would have been lost. I wouldn't have dared to slap mum into action or touch a naked young lady because of the fear of being sued.

As far as Sadie and myself were concerned, there were no options. The people who always know best what to do are never there when it matters, and we did what we thought was right and let common sense prevail.

A good few years after the cricket ball incident and young Mary's attempted suicide, I found myself back at the old

Accident and Emergency building at the Northern General Hospital to find that it had all changed. The wall clock inside the building showed 8.46am and I hadn't allowed for the lack of traffic because the schools were closed for half-term. I've always taken pride in the fact that I was never late for an appointment, and I would rather be one hour early than one minute late and now here I was sitting and waiting along with about twenty or so other people, and about fifteen minutes early.

I couldn't believe that I was here anyway, as I watched the clock tick on to 8.47am. Looking around me I thought how relaxed everyone looked, and here I was shuffling in my chair like a little kid. The room itself was basically the same and I remembered some of the reasons as to why I'd been here so many times before. It was usually as a result of fights, drunks, road-accident victims, sudden deaths and many other reasons. None of these reasons held fond memories and as I looked at the clock again it registered 8.50am.

The kids, Richard, Sally and Paul, would just about be having breakfast now with Christine. The little one, Paul, would be playing his mum up and getting into bother. He was a little bugger and now he is like a clone of me, poor lad, except that he doesn't smoke or drink.

Thinking of drink made me think that I must have been drunk to agree to have the vasectomy, or, as we say in

Barnsley, have us 'nuts nipped' and I shuffled in my seat again at the thought of it.

8.52am. I couldn't stop thinking about how we castrated Uncle Jack's pigs and I started to shudder.

8.55am. I'd been asked if I wanted a nurse to shave me. I wished I'd said yes, because when I did it myself, and having a bit of a belly, I couldn't see what I was doing properly. I cut myself to ribbons and to cap it all fell backwards into the bath as well.

8.59am. 'When that clock gets to 9.01am and I've not been called, I'm out of here like a flash.'

9.00 am. 'Mr Johnson,' someone shouted and I nearly passed out. I held my hand up as if I was in the classroom. 'Go in there, get undressed and put this on,' she said and she passed me a gown. I was shaking like a rabid dog but I did as I was told and walked back into the room.

'You've put it on back to front.' How was I to know? I knew that they would have to come in from the front, so it seemed sensible to leave the opening at the front! I changed it round and eventually managed to tie the knots at the back.

'Go through that door across the corridor and knock on the big door, okay?' If I'd had my clothes I'd have legged it, but I hadn't, so I knocked lightly on the door, which was opened.

My visions of two house bricks being banged together

with my nuts in between them were dispelled. I was in a proper operating theatre with a big round dish with lights on, hanging over a table.

'Climb on there, Mr Johnson.' I did as I was told and opened my eyes to look at 'the voice'. I couldn't believe it, it was Dr Witty Umpire from several years before. He remembered the day of the cricket match and kept chuckling about it as he sprayed at either side of my knackers.

'Not much margin for error here, Mr Johnson,' he said and set off chuckling again.

He was still chuckling when he cut one side and pulled something. 'I wish he'd stop chuckling,' I thought as he did the other side and when he pulled this time, my head moved forward at the same time. Another spray on either side and then he taped some wadding to me.

'That's it, Mr Johnson. All done. We'll send for a sample in a few weeks,' he said and with that he shook my hand and I went back into the other room after thanking him. I couldn't believe it when the clock only said 9.11am. So quick!

Just then another man walked into the changing room clutching a gown and he looked absolutely terrified and was shaking just like I had been about ten minutes ago. Now it was all over, I was feeling brave, and I felt sorry for the man and tried to calm him down.

'Nothing to it, pal, don't worry,' I said, but he was still shaking. Even though I was walking like John Wayne, with all the wadding, I continued, 'Look I can even dance,' and I did a little jig. We were both getting changed when he asked, 'Did it hurt?' The poor man was frightened so I said, 'No, they cut into my groin, and pulled the tube and then cut into the other side and then did the same.' I was just going to say, 'No problem at all', when the poor man fainted and slumped to the floor.

'Nurse, nurse,' I shouted, and in she rushed.

'What's happened? she asked, and when I told her she went crackers at me.

'He's only come in to have a couple of warts removed, like the rest of them here. No wonder he's fainted, poor man, you're the only vasectomy today.'

I felt dreadful, and the nurse shouted for the man's wife and ordered me out of the building. No wonder the rest of them looked relaxed – I thought they were all having their nuts nipped like me. It wasn't funny at the time and I felt awful, but if you were to ask me whether I've laughed about it since? The answer would be yes, many, many times.

I would like to dedicate this chapter to all the wonderful and caring doctors, nurses and ambulance crews in the country, but especially all those at hospitals in Sheffield, Rotherham and Barnsley, coupled with the names of my good friends and nurses themselves: Pam Walker, Gillian Touhey, Michelle Thompson and Helen Sergeant of the Northern General Hospital.

CHAPTER NINETEEN

What an Embarrassment

There is and never will be an easy way to do it. I have never seen or even heard of a textbook that offers guidance on the subject. Just to make our lives more difficult still, no one at the training department ever advised us on how to tackle this very delicate and important part of the job. If the call came and it appertained to your beat you were on your own, whether you had three months' service in or thirty years. In those days, communications weren't as good as they are today and the only scant piece of information that I'd been given was a name and address and the reason for my visit. All of us had done it several times before and people's reactions were very varied.

Knocking on the door of someone's house and telling them that a near relative had died was bad enough, but to tell someone that a near relative had been killed, either at work or in a road accident, is another matter altogether. To make this matter even worse, I had to inform someone that his brother, a member of the armed forces, had been blown up and killed by a bomb whilst trying to defuse it in order to save lives.

'What do you say, how do you say it and how would he react?' I thought to myself as I drove into the street where he lived.

Pulling up, I looked at the house numbers on the terraced road and worked out that the property concerned was ten houses down from me. Driving fairly slowly, I glanced at the house and then drove past. Standing and looking through the window was a big man looking agitated and angry and, at that moment, I knew that somehow he already knew. Further on and out of sight of the house I pulled up to talk to a man who was cleaning his car, and I ascertained from him that the deceased brother's children were at school and his wife would be at work. He also told me that the man I was going to see was very fit and very strong.

Leaving the car where it was, I slowly walked towards the house and saw the man still at the window. I took off my helmet and covered my heart with it for two reasons, one so that it would indicate the reason for my visit and two as a sign of respect and sympathy.

As he walked out of the back door and came towards me he said, 'I don't want to hear you tell me anything.' And then he kicked a low brick wall, knocking some of it down.

'I'm so sorry, but how did you know?'

'It was on the TV news at 1pm. They wouldn't name him until relatives had been informed, and when I saw you, I knew.' As he said it his fists were clenched, but I realised that it was anger and frustration that was coming out and that he meant me no harm.

'Perhaps a sedative might help. Shall I call a doctor?' I asked.

'No thanks, I'll deal with it on my own. Please leave.'

Back at the car, I asked the neighbour to keep an eye on him and off I went. No wonder the poor man was angry; but I understood his need to grieve on his own and I was satisfied in my own mind that he would be okay.

I left the house and got back in the police car feeling really bad after giving this man the bad news. You can't allow yourself to dwell on these things; they were all part of the job but a very upsetting part at that. I made my way back to Attercliffe police station for my snap in the knowledge that a bit of banter with the lads and, hopefully, a game of table tennis would lift my spirits.

Attercliffe police station was a fairly large building and we were lucky in that it had two snooker tables and one table-tennis table. We were allowed forty-five minutes' mealtime, so if you bolted down your snap you could manage a game or two. I loved table tennis and played a decent game and, like the other players, my ambition was to beat PC John Fryer, who was in a class of his own.

John hadn't even broken sweat, whereas I was sweating like a boiled turnip and was way behind him in the game as usual. Suddenly there was quite a racket coming from the front of the building so we had to pack it in, and we all dashed out to see what was happening.

Running down the corridor, I could see a man lying on the floor looking as though he'd done twelve rounds with Muhammad Ali. Held with string around his neck was a piece of white card and on it was written: 'This is the dirty b —— d who molested ———— .'

It didn't mean anything to me but it must have done to someone and he was arrested. It seems that a car had pulled up in front of the nick and the man, or should I say pillock, had been thrown through the swing doors of the police station. There was no messing about back then and I'll bet that when he got to prison there would be no shortage of volunteers to gently teach him the error of his ways. 'Oh dear, what a shame,' I thought.

Attacks like this and the mugging of old people were fairly rare and, if the public caught the perpetrator before we did, this is the sort of thing that would happen.

*

After that, there was no time left for table tennis because there was a new sergeant to Attercliffe, Reg Hickman, and he needed to be shown around the different beats within the Division and, at the same time, get to know us as individuals. I was working a car beat in the Tinsley area and he chose to work with me for the next three hours. It was a hot summer and we were both in shirtsleeve order, which made us feel a bit cooler.

The huge Tinsley viaduct was due to open in a few months and as we drove near to it we both marvelled at its construction. In those days the only way to cross the River Don was via Weedon Street and, as we headed back in that direction, I saw in front of us a BSA 250cc motorbike being ridden erratically by what I thought, at first, was a young boy. Following him down Weedon Street, I saw him turn right towards Rotherham and he was all over the road.

Coming alongside him with the blue light flashing, I expected to see a pair of short trousers, but it was in fact a small youth of about eighteen. As we pulled him in he just smiled and the cheeky little bugger even waved. I'd seen more life in a tramp's vest than I had in this lad, and he just sat on the bike totally unconcerned as I approached him on foot. He wasn't the size of two pen'orth of copper and, just as I stood looking down at him on the motorbike seat, I got a shock. With both his feet on the footrests of the bike he suddenly stood up and at the same time hit me full in the mouth with his little fist. I was speechless and couldn't believe what had happened. I could taste blood and in the split second that I stood there he put the bike in gear and was off, waving and laughing as he went.

Both my lips were split but I was more embarrassed than hurt. I've decked some big men in my time, but Tiny Tim took me by complete surprise and, if the other lads found out what had happened, I'd be in for some right stick.

It had all happened in the blink of an eye almost and the sergeant was now out of the car laughing hysterically. I felt a right twerp and even though my pride was hurt I was also laughing as we set off after him.

The Sergeant was laughing his head off and kept saying, 'He was only as big as three shirt buttons.' I knew I had to grin and bear it but even if we caught the lad I couldn't get my own back – he was too small for that.

As he turned into Alsing Road, which was a dead end then, I thought we'd got him, but he shot through the entranceway of what seemed to be some works and he was off again. It had been sunny for weeks and, as we followed him, he was kicking up loads of sandy-coloured dust and it was difficult to see him. After another half a mile of this, the car was covered in the stuff and the sergeant shouted, 'Have you farted?'

'No,' I replied. 'I thought it was you.'

After another 100 yards the car slowed down to a stop and

we could neither go forwards nor backwards. The car was covered in very thick dust and when I opened the door, I could see that we were stuck up to the axles in the stuff.

'Where are we?' asked Sergeant Hickman.

'In the bloody s — t, that's where!' I replied.

Forty years ago there was a very large tract of land lying at the side of the River Don and behind what is now Magna. It stretched from the two milk bottles (two cooling towers which have now been demolished) at the side of what is now the M1 motorway, right across to the edge of Rotherham, maybe a mile away. Situated on this tract of land was a huge sewage treatment plant, the entrance to which we must have driven through when following Tiny Tim. It was on this land that all the processed excrement was spread out to dry prior to its removal. Luckily things have changed since then, but that is where we ended up that day, right bang in the middle of it all. The lad on the bike got away and we had to radio for assistance and our stinking police car, which was now brown instead of white, was dragged out by a tractor with us still in it.

Reg turned out to be a good sergeant and every time we bump into each other he'll say, 'Do you remember that day when we landed in the s — t?'

I took some stick off the lads, which is what I expected, and as I walked through the office one day I heard the inspector say, 'There's a playground fight at the infant school, send for Martyn Johnson.' Everyone, including me, laughed: it was all part of the banter that created a fantastic bond between us. Having said that, if ever I get my hands on Tiny Tim, I'll bury him up to the neck in that horrible brown dust.

A couple of weeks after this I was working the same car beat again, but this time on night shift. For the first two hours I was working with Sergeant Plonker, who would do anybody for anything just to get on. He wasn't my cuppa tea at all and I drove him round all the obscure places on my beat in the hope that he'd get fed up. 'I'm told that you know where rabbits live – do you?' Thinking he was trying to catch me out or something I said, 'Yes, in burrows.'

'No, I mean to see one for real, like now, while we're working.' I didn't trust him at all and was wary about my answer.

'Why do you ask, Sergeant?' I asked politely.

'Because I've never seen one in my life, not wild ones, anyway.' I realised that he was serious and drove the short distance to the top of Wincobank Hill and down towards the Romano-British fort.

It didn't take long to catch one in the headlamp beam and as I did so he shouted, 'Stop.' As I stopped, he jumped out of the car, drew his truncheon and, much to my amusement, started to chase the rabbit. Now you know why I called him Sergeant Plonker. The rabbit zigged and zagged and, by the time he came back to the car empty-handed, he was puffing and panting like a good 'un.

'I've only ever seen one hop before now; I didn't know that they could run like that,' he said as he plonked himself back in the car and, thankfully, nodded off for an hour as I slowly shook my head in disbelief.

I was glad to be on my own again after snap time, and with only two and a half hours to go I was thinking about my breakfast when the radio went: 'Attend Meadowhall Road, where a lorry has hit a bridge.'

'Roger, over and out,' I replied and I was off. I'd spoken too soon about a quiet night, but with nothing on the road at this time in a morning, how has a lorry run into a bridge?

Pulling up at the scene, I could see the large lorry with a man standing beside it and he seemed to be okay. At that time there were two very narrow, low bridges on Meadowhall Road and the lorry was stuck under one of them, having misjudged the height. The driver was unhurt and very apologetic. 'How did you manage to do this?' I asked.

'I must have missed the sign which said "low bridge" back up the road,' he answered.

'Is there much damage?'

At this point he led me round to the other side of the vehicle and pointed. With the aid of my torch I could see that the whole side of the lorry had been ripped open as it had tried to get through the narrow bridge. Flashing the torch further on, I stopped dead in my tracks. There, covering the width of the road, were twenty tons of fresh green peas, which had been destined for Batchelor's Foods Factory in Hillsborough.

Blocking the road off with the police car, I went back to Mr Pod the pea man (the driver) and reported him for careless driving, and then radioed for Road Traffic to attend the scene. I also asked that the City Cleansing Department be informed in order for them to remove the huge amount of peas from the road.

Now twenty tons of peas is a lot of peas and, as Mr Pod said, they would now be condemned as unfit for human consumption. What a waste. So I radioed the nick to inform them of the situation. An ambulance crew had also been asked to attend the scene and quite a few men from the nearby steelworks had walked across for a nosey.

It was a free-for-all and the driver gave the ambulance crew and ourselves some carrier bags which he had in his cab and people were just helping themselves knowing that if they didn't, the peas would be dumped at the nearest tip. The two men from the Cleansing Department had only one shovel each and the road was closed for most of the day until both the lorry and its contents were finally removed.

Within half an hour it was like the Californian gold rush, but in this case it was a pea rush. Buckets, haversacks, snap tins, bottles, flat caps and even a works barrow, all were utilised to try to reduce the vast amount of fresh peas that hadn't touched the road.

At about 6.30am I was approached by a couple of men from the steelworks who were carrying an empty bucket each. Thinking that they were going to ask if it was okay to help themselves to the peas I got quite a surprise when one of them said, 'I've just seen a body floating in the river over there', and he pointed to the River Don.

'Are you serious?' I asked.

'Yes, I'll show you where it is.' So off we went, along with one of the Road Traffic lads.

The man was right and from near the edge of the sloping riverbank I could see the naked body of a man nudging up to a bed of reeds. The majority of people who commit suicide by drowning, for some reason remove their clothing before doing so. It was therefore likely that this would turn out to be a suicide victim.

The body, going on experience, looked as if it had been in the water for some time and could well have been stuck in the reeds for weeks. I couldn't quite reach it, so, with a knife borrowed from the chap from the steelworks, I cut some thin branches from a nearby willow tree. If I could get him out of the reed bed and to the riverbank, the Road Traffic lad and myself could drag him out, with a bit of luck.

After prodding, poking and pushing the body and nearly

falling in the river twice, I managed to dislodge him from the reed bed with the help of the tree branches. Just as I was punting the body into the bankside, the branch snapped and I very nearly landed on top of him in the river. I had one leg in the water and, as the Road Traffic lad grabbed my arm to pull me out I heard him shout, '————— hell, look at that!'

As I turned I could see that the body, having been released from the reed bed, was now being swept gently along by the current in the direction of Rotherham. To my horror and dismay I could also see a four-foot length of wood sticking up out of the body and I also swore. The piece of wood must have got stuck between the poor man's ribs and there was nothing I could do about it, but watch.

Back then, Rotherham had its own police force, seperate to ours, and when I got back to Attercliffe nick I contacted them, telling them to expect a visitor and also how to recognise him. There was nothing I could do, these things unfortunately happen. I signed off duty, having done another two hours unpaid overtime and went to bed.

At 11pm that night I was back at work, where I was told to phone the head of Rotherham CID which I did immediately.

'PC 656 Johnson, sir,' I said.

'We've recovered a body from the River Don in Rotherham earlier today.'

'Yes, sir.'

'It looked as though Robin Hood had been using it for archery practice, it's full of holes. What can you tell me about it?'

I wanted to laugh at what he'd said but daren't as I explained my earlier actions to him and the reason for the holes in the body, which I wasn't surprised at.

'That explains that, then. He was reported missing from home in Sheffield about ten weeks ago and the pathologist thinks that he's been dead in the water all that time. Right, thank you.'

If it hadn't been for the lorry and its load of peas, the body could have remained undiscovered in the reed bed for a long time, so at least the poor family knew a lot sooner what had become of him, which I'm sure was more comfort to them than not knowing at all.

Like all the lads on our shift I was sick to the back teeth of eating peas, and we didn't need motorbikes or cars; we were all jet-propelled for weeks afterwards.

CHAPTER TWENTY

9am Monday Morning . . .

'Morning, Frank, make a note of these please. Saw Norman —— driving a green minivan registration number ABC 123 along Attercliffe Road towards Rotherham at 10.40am. 11.06am saw Harold —— pushing an empty wheelbarrow near to derelict houses on Oaks Green. His intentions were obvious but when he saw me he legged it. 9.20am stopped and checked Ford pick-up registered number —— being driven by Gerald —— for stolen metal. 8.10am saw Bill Bloggs outside —— scrapyard on Stevenson Road.'

Before the advent of police radios and mobile phones, our only way to keep tabs on the activities of local criminals was to collate any information or sightings of them at the collator's office in Whitworth Lane Police Station. The collators' office was usually manned by either PC Frank Cooper or PC Stan Jones and on this occasion the collator was Frank Cooper, who said, 'Thanks, Martyn and by the way, there've been a few reports coming in of scrap metal being nicked from various places around the city over the weekend. Also keep an eye out for John ———— who's been seen in a pick-up truck registered number ———— .'

By exchanging information with each other we were able to keep up to date, to some degree, with what was going off and I never forgot the old sergeant's words when he said that arresting one prisoner for crime was the equivalent to the reporting of a hundred motorists. Those few words were like music to my ears and over a period of time I learned that if you caught them bang to rights it was a lot less hassle, and they invariably pleaded guilty at court.

To be classed as a criminal you obviously had to have committed a crime, but not all criminals are caught and they are, therefore, classed as suspected criminals as opposed to convicted criminals. Crime itself can vary from petty to serious and the people who commit crime can range from kids to old people, whilst their motives for doing so in the first place vary tremendously.

Sunday mornings were nearly always quiet, with most people having a lie-in after a week's hard graft. I was walking the beat in an area that was removed from the grime of the east end of the city, and in the warm sunshine of early May the birds were singing their little heads off. Chicks had been hatched and some of them, like the blackbirds, would be fully fledged and fending for themselves, allowing mum and dad to get ready for the second clutch to arrive.

After seven years on the beat I'd found many a cuppa-tea spot and I was whistling to myself as I walked into the paper shop on Richmond Road at about 7.30am. Fifteen minutes and a mug of tea later I was saying thanks and cheerio to Alf, the shopkeeper, when in walked a young lady.

'A pint of milk please, Alf, that old man's nicked mine from off the back step – again.'

'You're the third one to complain this morning,' said Alf as he passed her a bottle of milk and looked to me at the same time. I, like all the other lads working our Division, knew who the lady was talking about, it had been happening over a period of several years. Like ourselves, everyone felt sorry for the poor old man who lived alone and no one would make an official complaint about him so we were powerless to act.

He must have been in his late seventies, but he'd have beaten 'Ernie' as the fastest milkman in the West. As the milk was delivered to the various doorsteps in the area, the old man would follow and then quickly 'borrow' one or two bottles for himself. Because he 'borrowed' the milk from different houses on the various different housing estates in his locality, no one realised the extent of the offences committed because of the lack of complaints.

Earlier I'd arranged to meet the sergeant at the police box and, after discussion, it was decided that, for the sake of the old chap himself and the people in the locality, something had to be done, even though no one had made a complaint against him.

As the side door of the house opened in response to our knocking, the smell of sour milk hit us in a big way and unwashed empty milk bottles could be seen everywhere – what a sight. The sergeant played his cards brilliantly and told the nice old chap that the Co-op Dairy was running out of milk bottles and asked him if he minded them being returned.

'Am I in trouble?' asked the old chap nervously.

'No, but the Dairy is – they've no bottles left,' replied the sergeant.

'They can have mine then, I buy them from the paper shop but forget to take the empties back,' and he chuckled to himself in obvious relief. At this point, the sergeant left in order to arrange with the Co-op Dairy on Broughton Lane for the collection of the milk bottles from the old chap's house.

'Come on in if you can get in,' said old Ernie. 'Do you want a mug of tea?'

Anyone who knows me will tell you that I am a proper tea belly and I was as dry as a bone, but having seen mice running everywhere in the kitchen and all the mouldy green milk bottles, I politely declined the old man's offer.

The smell was horrendous and I sat outside on the back step and waited for the lorry to arrive and remove the empty bottles.

'Come to pick up a few milk bottles, Officer,' said the driver of the lorry when he arrived.

'Judging from what I saw when I looked into the kitchen, I think you may well be surprised. Let's have a proper look,' I replied and in we went. It was amazing.

'Old Ernie' had got some bottle all right, and I was later told by the Dairy that the final count was just short of 6,000. How can you live in a house with 6,000 empty and unwashed milk bottles? Ernie was delighted at the clear-out of his house and he kept finding things that he'd not seen for years, like his cap, a wireless, a new pair of shoes and even his old pipe. On the Monday morning I got in touch with Social Services, who arranged for the house to be fumigated. When I next saw Alf in the paper shop he told me that Ernie was now a different person, as if a load had been taken off his mind – which of course it had!

In my early days on the job serious crimes against a person, such as murder, rape or robbery with violence were fairly rare and I believe that one of the reasons why this was the case was due to the fact that all of us on the job, from rooky bobby up to the big boss himself, the Chief Constable, took it as a personal insult that someone had dared to commit such a crime in our city and as a result of this every one of us put 100 per cent effort into catching the perpetrators.

Computers, DNA and advanced forensic science were unavailable to us then, and for major crimes we relied heavily upon house-to-house enquiries, local knowledge, information from the public and our own individual network of 'talkative' people from within the criminal underworld. A police incident room would be set up in a convenient building near to the scene of the crime and this would be manned by a telephonist, typist, collator and several members of CID including an officer in charge.

One day, many years ago, I was working a beat in a certain area of the city when I was asked to attend an address to where an ambulance had been summoned for an unknown reason. Calls like this were not unusual and you never knew the reason for the call until you got there.

The ambulance had just arrived and I followed the crew up the passageway to the back door of the house which was wide open even though it was bitterly cold.

Standing in front of us in the off-shot kitchen was an old lady wearing a long pinafore. She had her arms wrapped around a young girl aged about eight years old, whose face was as white as driven snow and she was shaking. She was staring in front of her with a blank expression on her face. Looking further at the girl I could see that the inside of both her legs, below her skirt, were covered in fresh blood, as were her little white ankle socks. The old lady whispered to me what I'd already worked out. Not only had the poor little girl been raped, but the evil bastard who'd done it had threatened her with a knife before brutalising her further.

A few seconds later the poor little mite's distraught mother arrived, having been informed by the old lady's neighbour and in less than four minutes of our arrival the girl and mum were on their way to hospital.

Having told the old lady that I would be back shortly, I ran to the telephone box about half a mile away and phoned the station asking for assistance to be sent to the scene. A policewoman was despatched to the hospital to interview the poor little girl and I went back to the house. Within ten minutes the Hillman Husky and the inspector arrived, along with the CID lads and then, later, the police dog-handler attended.

An incident room was set up in a nearby library and the detective in charge later got us together for a briefing. He informed us that the little girl had been walking home from a local shop when she was grabbed by a man with wild eyes who was brandishing a large knife. His hand was over her mouth as he dragged her to a nearby garage site where the rape took place. As he told us about her injuries and what had happened to her, I could see her in my mind's eye standing in the kitchen several hours before and I realised that without thinking, both my hands had formed a fist and I would have loved a 'not-so-quiet' chat with the monster that was responsible for ruining her life for ever. I consoled myself, as I'm sure did the other lads, that at least the girl was alive; she could quite easily have been murdered that day.

The old lady who'd phoned the ambulance had heard the girl sobbing after her ordeal and had taken her to her own home, not knowing at that time where the little girl lived.

Several of us uniform lads did house-to-house enquiries, taking statements and establishing people's whereabouts at the relevant times and the details were then collated and sifted through by the CID lads for any clues. There was no paid overtime then and, as the incident had made a national newspaper, policemen from outside the city were calling the incident room to offer to work their two days off in order to help with the enquiry. What about that for dedication?

I was only on the fringe of the enquiry, but about a week later it had become pretty obvious who the culprit was from the evidence gathered by the CID. Witnesses had seen the suspect near to the crime scene both before and shortly after the rape. As the girl had said, he had wild eyes and he was also seen to be brandishing a knife. Enquiries had ascertained that he had been released from a mental institution and that he was totally unfit to be interviewed. He was later registered as insane and returned to the institution and for this reason there was no option but to close the case.

The little girl's face when I saw her that day will haunt me for ever and over the years I have only seen her twice from a distance. The expression on her face was still the same and the events of that day will be with her for the rest of her life. How could anyone do such a thing?

'Johnson, there's a bloke at the front desk (office) asking to talk to you,' said the sergeant.

'Who is it, Sarge?' I asked.

'I don't know, but he says he'll only talk to you,' he replied. I had only been on the job a couple of years at this time and had just finished my snap in the morning break at Attercliffe police station.

Walking up the corridor, I could see a young man of about thirty pacing up and down and looking rather anxious. I didn't know him from Adam and introduced myself. 'How can I help you?' I asked.

'I don't trust coppers and I have not been out of prison long for thieving.'

'So why do you want to speak to me then?' I asked.

'I know a couple of blokes who have broken into different places, stole some shotguns and then used them in armed robberies and you lads are going mad trying to find them.'

'What's this leading up to?' I asked.

'I know where they are holed up; they are armed with revolvers and shotguns and will use them if approached.'

'I'd better get someone from CID.'

'No way! I nicked a load of metal from work and they got me eighteen months, I am not telling them anything.'

'Why tell me then? I don't even know you.' I said, and at this point he looked to be rather nervous.

'Do you remember about eighteen months ago you arrested my father-in-law for stealing coal?'

I shook my head slowly and then I suddenly remembered the old man. 'Yes, I do, why?'

'After I'd gone to prison my wife and baby son were left on their own with nothing, until you helped them out. I don't agree with shooters and this will be the first and last time that I will grass anyone up – it's my way of saying thank you to you for what you did for us – okay?' (see Chapter 1, *What's Tha Up To?*)

I wrote down the two names and the address that he gave me and with that he opened the police-station door and was gone. I never saw him again. The two names meant nothing to me, but upstairs in the CID office it was a very different story.

Both the men were wanted for a series of armed robberies in the Midlands and the north of England and it later transpired that the address I had been given was that of a man strongly suspected of committing serious crime, the house itself being situated in a village near Manchester. On several occasions they had evaded police capture and, as the man had told me, they were at the top of the 'most wanted' list. For my part, having passed on the information to the necessary department, that was the end of it until a couple of weeks later when I was told that three men had been arrested after an armed siege at the house. Several firearms and a load of stolen property had been recovered and the men were later sent to prison for a very long time.

During my first seven or eight years on the beat, I had made quite a few decent arrests and had been awarded several commendations from both the Chief Constable and court judges for a job well done. If you don't listen, you learn nowt and with the aid of a big ear, common sense, observations and a bit of gumption the arrests were made. Like the old sergeant had told me a few years before: 'One good prisoner is worth more than reporting a hundred motorists and is easier to deal with as well.'

It was 8.40am on Monday morning and I was walking down Whitworth Lane towards the police station. Two or three ladies were sitting on their upstairs window ledges, washing their sash windows with their backs facing towards the street and their feet still inside the house and on the bedroom floor. It looked dangerous to me, what if they fell? But that is the way it was done back then.

Mrs Webster, who lived opposite the nick, was scouring her front step but looked up when she saw me. 'You look smart today, love, in that suit, where's your uniform?'

Three days prior to this I had been told by the duty

inspector to report at 9am on Monday morning at Attercliffe police station. I was to become a Detective Constable and here I was, in a borrowed suit, about to report for duty. Questions were in my mind when I arrived for work. Would I fit in? Would I like or hate the job? I loved the beat and the people that I met and knew on it – would I miss them?

'Welcome to the CID, Martyn,' said Detective Sergeant Mick Smith, a great guy who was both comical and also very astute. 'Let me introduce you to the team.'

And what a team of characters they turned out to be . . .

Thanks for reading the book and I hope you found it interesting. If I live a bit longer I'll let you know how I got on in CID by telling you some more unusual and funny stories. All the best, and I'll meet you in my next book.

Please note that some of the names and places mentioned above have been changed for privacy reasons.

Honour Amongst Thieves

It was a gorgeous summer's morning as my wife Christine and I drove along the Stocksbridge bypass in the direction of Manchester and the beautiful moors surrounding the Woodhead Pass, which meanders over the Pennine Hills. Just before a favourite pub of mine, the Dog and Partridge, run by Steve and his wife Audrey, we turned left onto a track leading to a lovely stone house situated on the very edge of the heather moors.

Christine is a beekeeper and has about ten hives containing approximately 500,000 bees. During the spring months her beehives are kept in the parkland of Wentworth Woodhouse, the largest house in England. There, the bees collect pollen from the wild flowers in the area and from the oilseed rape which grows in the easily recognisable large yellow fields surrounding Wentworth. When this crop dies off, the bees are then sealed in their hives and transported to the chalky soil of Beverley and Humberside, where a small blue flower called borage is cultivated. The bees are required to pollinate the plants and this takes about four to five weeks. At the same time as the borage flowers die off, the heather on the moors on Woodhead just begins to bloom, and so the bees are once more transported, this time to an area behind John, the moor-keeper's house, where they forage on the heather, starting in early August.

We got to the house and Christine gave John a couple of jars of spring honey to keep him going until September when the heather started to bloom. I love the moors and after chatting to John for a while about wildlife we were on our way again.

The county boundary of Yorkshire and Derbyshire is a short distance before Saltersbrook bridge, which was part of an ancient routeway used for thousands of years by the salters who carried salt across the moors from the naturally occurring salt pans of Nantwich, Middlewich, Horwich and Northwich, in Cheshire. Salt was a valuable commodity and the packhorse trains that carried it would have taken it to places like Barnsley, Sheffield, Rotherham and Hull, from where some of it would have been transported to Rome itself. Part of a Roman soldier's pay was in salt, which is where the word 'salary' originates. The name Psalter Lane seen in both Sheffield and Rotherham refers to the old original salt roads.

It was at this point that we turned right and headed towards Winscar Reservoir, which was about two miles down the road and our destination for the day.

A few weeks prior to this, 25 June 2009, my mate Stephen Fletcher, a serving police officer, had told me that there was to be a mock air crash in the area of Winscar Reservoir which would allow the emergency services to practise their skills in the recovery of survivors. It would also mean they could collate all the information from lessons learned during the exercise, thus helping to formulate plans and strategies that would enable the services to be prompt, efficient and capable should it unfortunately occur for real at some time in the future. All in all, a major exercise and a logistical nightmare.

BBC Radio Sheffield informed the public that they could attend and watch proceedings from various vantage points and so, having nothing better to do, Christine and I set off fairly early to avoid the rush and enjoy a day with a difference in the sunshine.

On our arrival at the massive dam-head wall we could see people being hauled up on ropes clutching bodies with, what I later learned, forensic scientists waiting to take over the bodies at the top of the wall. Blue flashing lights were everywhere and we were directed further up the valley to a small road that ran along the side of the reservoir and about half a mile from the dam head.

A young policewoman flagged us down and explained to us that, the day before, part of an aeroplane fuselage had been sunk in the reservoir along with dummy bodies, suitcases and hand luggage. Dummy bodies and body parts were also strewn on the moors waiting to be recovered by mountain rescue teams and forensic experts. All find spots had to be recorded and mapped in order to assist the air-crash investigators at a later stage. After thanking her for the information I asked where we could park. I expected hundreds of people to be there already, but we seemed to be the first. The policewoman said we could park anywhere on the left past a fairly large cut into the cliff face which was taped off. If the police helicopter came, this was the only place where it could land.

Aeroplanes and helicopters have always fascinated me and so I parked up near to where the chopper would land – if it came at all.

There was so much to see. To our left near the dam wall were policemen carrying bodies on stretchers. Forensic teams, dressed in yellow plastic body suits, were labelling up all that was brought to them, including the body pieces from up in the hills as well as odd bits of luggage. In front of us was a small but fast police motor launch like the ones on the River Thames. Near to this were two rubber dinghies containing frogmen, and in the water itself you could see bubbles rising to the surface coming from the aqualungs of the divers who were searching the dark waters below. Every now and then a body or a suitcase would be brought to the surface and transferred to the police launch, which would take them to the dam head.

After about an hour, we got the picnic table and chairs out and walked nearer to the water's edge. It being June, the water level had dropped dramatically and the bank was quite steep. To our right I spotted a small piece of flatter land on the bankside near to a large boulder, which must have come from the quarry behind us, perfect for a picnic and the boulder gave us a bit of shade from the boiling-hot sun.

We enjoyed a nice two or three hours with our snap and *The Times* crossword, interspersed with watching the divers and also the abundant wildlife. We fed the ducks and ducklings as well as the Canada geese and their goslings. Through my binoculars I watched the curlews and snipe on the opposite hill and felt at peace with the world. I think we must have dozed off when suddenly we were woken by the unmistakable thud, thud, thud of a helicopter's rotor blades clawing at the air.

I was galvanised into action. I jumped up like a six-year-old kid and shouted Christine to get the camera. Excitement on my part would be an understatement. I couldn't wait to see it, but whichever way I looked there was nothing. We moved out from behind the rock just as the police helicopter was approaching its landing place. It was coming straight at us at a height of about fifty feet. What a beautiful sight to see. Then in a split second I thought we were in a tornado. We were showered with grit, flies and dried bird s — t and, as my glasses shot off my head, I could see the picnic, picnic table and chairs fly past me down the bank and to the reservoir below. The power of the chopper was awesome. A couple of seconds later it was all over and we just stood there, speechless. At first there was a strange silence except for the helicopter rotor blades slowly getting quieter.

Someone passed me my glasses and I thought I'd gone blind in my right eye until I realised that there was a big lump of goose s —— t on the lens.

Three men in uniform jumped from the helicopter and ran the fifty yards or so towards us and I thought that we were in serious trouble for being so near to the landing site. From us waking up in our chairs to now had taken less than a minute.

'My name is Captain Doug Hale and I am the pilot of the police helicopter. The only way that I could land in the quarry was to come around the back of the hill. I'm very sorry that you caught some of the downdraught but we didn't see you until it was too late to alter our course,' said Captain Hale, apologetically.

'It's me that should be sorry,' I answered. 'We've innocently strayed into your flight path. No one could see us from the road so no one knew we were there and you couldn't have seen us until we moved from behind that big rock.' I don't know who was more relieved, the Captain or me.

We must have looked a right sight, covered in dust and bird s — t. Several people had gathered around us and the frogmen were recovering our table and chairs from the reservoir. The ducks were finishing the remains of our snap and, even though it may have been inappropriate, we couldn't stop laughing.

'Would you and your wife like to look at the aircraft?' asked Captain Hale. Would I! I'd have given my right arm to look at it. What a question, and what a privilege.

We were introduced to the two air observers, PC Adrian Pogmore and PC Matt Lucas and the three officers told us all about the workings and capabilities of the aircraft. We had our pictures taken with the crew who, along with everyone else we met that day, were kindness itself and a credit to the South Yorkshire Police Force and its Chief Constable 'Med' Hughes.

I'd left my car windows open for the day and it was now full of dust and spiders by the hundred, presumably brought down in the draught from the helicopter – amazing. When the aircraft left it flew around the reservoir and then came towards us and the other spectators and dipped its nose as if saying cheerio. Everyone clapped in appreciation. A great public relations job – well done lads!

It's not every day that a helicopter nearly lands on your head, but we had a thoroughly enjoyable day out and were happy.

On our drive home I couldn't stop thinking how times had changed since I joined the old Sheffield City Police Force in 1962, about fifty years ago. Then it was a totally different world to today, as those who have read my first book *What's Tha Up To?* will already know. The one divisional car, the Hillman Husky Shooting Brake, has been replaced by a shared divisional helicopter and high-powered patrol cars. Our line of communication – the public payphone – has been replaced by walkie-talkies and mobile phones and our fifteen-inch piece of wood (the truncheon) has been replaced by batons, CS gas and sometimes guns, whilst the uniforms themselves are covered by stab-proof vests and sometimes body armour, riot helmets and riot shields.

I agree totally with all these new innovations, they are unfortunately necessary in this modern world that we live in. There is no escape from the helicopter, and the communications systems and fast cars allow policemen to be on the job quicker. Policemen need to be safe and able to defend themselves when the need arises. I'm all for that.

Gone are the old days when I had to ride a pedal cycle furiously from Attercliffe Common to Prince of Wales Road (about two miles) to deal with a road traffic accident because the Hillman Husky divisional car was tied up on another job.

A young newly-married couple had swerved to miss a child crossing the road and had subsequently hit a concrete lamp standard. Unfortunately for the young couple, the lamp standard broke and fell on top of the car, killing them both instantly. Being local to the Manor area, both lots of parents were at the scene on my arrival. There were people trying, without success, to get the couple out of the car and both sets of parents were, understandably, hysterical. Dealing with a double fatal accident is not easy, especially when you are on your own. Where do you begin? What do you do first? The parents' grief was bad enough but, to make matters worse, when the bodies were eventually recovered from the car, the parents discovered that both matching wedding rings and matching watches had been stolen from the bodies.

Today, modern, improved communications and police fast-response cars could not have prevented the tragedy, but may well have prevented the despicable theft of the wedding rings and watches and the further pain inflicted on the already grieving parents.

I later put the word out to some of the local 'likely' lads who were very indignant when told the story. No self-respecting thief would do such a thing. If you had been right with them then, in circumstances like this, they would be right with you, and the words 'Tell them poor parents that we'll get the b ——— d' were all the words I wanted to hear. It was a long shot, but maybe it would work, I would have to wait and see.

A few days later a man walked into Attercliffe Police Station, admitted the offence and at the same time handed in the rings and watches. Apparently he had tried to sell them for £5 to one of the 'likely' lads. Summary justice in the form of a beating had taken place, as could be seen by the man's two black eyes and several missing teeth. He had been ordered to go to the police station with the rings and watches in the knowledge that if he didn't, there was more to come. Good old-fashioned bobbying had prevailed and won the day. It must have been a huge relief to the poor parents of the dead couple to have something to treasure at a time when they needed it most.

A good regular beat bobby, wherever they were in the country, knew most people on his patch or beat and just as importantly, they knew him. Like a vicar you had a flock to watch over, even in a city. To that flock you were sometimes a mother or father, teacher, doctor, social worker, guardian, advisor, agony aunt and many other professions all rolled into one. To them, once you had their trust, brought about by long-term mutual respect, you were part of their lives and more important to them than the Chief Constable. They knew where to find their bobby if they were in bother and conversely, you knew where to find them if they'd done wrong.

A stern word or a little clip coupled with a warning was much more effective and appreciated than a court appearance.

Our instructions or duties were the protection of life and property and the prevention and detection of crime. A good regular beat bobby must by his or her very presence stop lots of petty crime taking place, thus saving hundreds of man hours in its detection; and also creating a safer environment to live in for the local community.

In my opinion, being part of a loving, disciplined family who teach children to respect and help their elders from an early age is all-important. Discipline and being thoughtful towards others teaches us respect for each other. Without gizmos, gadgets and electronic games we made our own fun, and there was virtually no peer pressure or school bullying as there is today. Both teachers and policemen are paid to do a job and, unlike today, we were allowed to get on with it by using common sense and a bit of give and take. The threat of the cane or a 'cuff' from the bobby for scrumping apples now evokes memories of a happy childhood. I knew, as did my friends, that, for all the threats, they had our well-being at heart and I remember our local bobby and my teachers with respect.

Unfortunately for me, I am at an age where I can compare

then and now. Although I don't get involved in politics, I will say, 'Do everyone a favour and bring back our regular long-term beat bobby.' It would make such a massive difference to society in general and make our country a safer place to live in. Respect is hard-earned and easily lost and only by working among people and with people can respect for one another be achieved. Try it – it works.

Other bestselling titles available by mail

☐ What's Tha Up To?	Martyn Johnson	£6.99

The prices shown above are correct at time of going to press. However, the publishers reserve the right to increase prices on covers from those previously advertised, without further notice.

─────────────── sphere ───────────────

Please allow for postage and packing: **Free UK delivery**.
Europe: add 25% of retail price; Rest of World: 45% of retail price.

To order any of the above or any other Sphere titles, please call our credit card orderline or fill in this coupon and send/fax it to:

Sphere, PO Box 121, Kettering, Northants NN14 4ZQ
Fax: 01832 733076   Tel: 01832 737526
Email: aspenhouse@FSBDial.co.uk

☐ I enclose a UK bank cheque made payable to Sphere for £ . . . .
☐ Please charge £ . . . . to my Visa/Delta/Maestro

☐☐☐☐☐☐☐☐☐☐☐☐☐☐☐☐☐☐

Expiry Date ☐☐☐☐   Maestro Issue No. ☐☐

NAME (BLOCK LETTERS please) . . . .
ADDRESS . . . .
. . . .
. . . .
Postcode . . . . Telephone . . . .
Signature . . . .

Please allow 28 days for delivery within the UK. Offer subject to price and availability.